Credits

This Resource Guide, and the software desc[...]
Agreement, which is included with the produ[...]
prohibited uses.

Trademarks

Serif is a registered trademark of Serif (Europe) Ltd.

WebPlus is a registered trademark of Serif (Europe) Ltd.

All Serif product names are trademarks of Serif (Europe) Ltd.

Microsoft, Windows, and the Windows logo are registered trademarks of Microsoft Corporation. All other trademarks acknowledged.

Windows Vista and the Windows Vista Start button are trademarks or registered trademarks of Microsoft Corporation in the United States and/or other countries.

Copyrights

Digital Images ©2008 Hemera Technologies Inc. All Rights Reserved.

Digital Images ©2008 Jupiterimages Corporation, All Rights Reserved.

Digital Images ©2008 Jupiterimages France SAS, All Rights Reserved.

Content ©2008 Jupiterimages Corporation. All Rights Reserved.

Portions images ©1997-2002 Nova Development Corporation; ©1995 Expressions Computer Software; ©1996-98 CreatiCom, Inc.; ©1996 Cliptoart; ©1997 Multimedia Agency Corporation; ©1997-98 Seattle Support Group. Rights of all parties reserved.

Portions graphics import/export technology © AccuSoft Corp. &Eastman Kodak Company& LEAD Technologies, Inc.

THE PROXIMITY HYPHENATION SYSTEM © 1989 Proximity Technology Inc. All rights reserved.

THE PROXIMITY/COLLINS DATABASE® © 1990 William Collins Sons & Co. Ltd.; © 1990 Proximity Technology Inc. All rights reserved.

THE PROXIMITY/MERRIAM-WEBSTER DATABASE® © 1990 Merriam-Webster Inc.; © 1990 Proximity Technology Inc. All rights reserved.

The Sentry Spelling-Checker Engine © 2000 Wintertree Software Inc.

The ThesDB Thesaurus Engine © 1993-97 Wintertree Software Inc.

WGrammar Grammar-Checker Engine © 1998 Wintertree Software Inc.

Andrei Stcherbatchenko, Ferdinand Prantl

eBay © 1995-2008 eBay Inc. All Rights Reserved.

PayPal © 1999-2008 PayPal. All rights reserved.

Roman Cart © 2008 Roman Interactive Ltd. All rights reserved.

Mal's © 1998 to 2003 Mal's e-commerce Ltd. All rights reserved.

WebPlus X5
Resource Guide

Contacting Serif

Contacting Serif technical support

Our support mission is to provide fast, friendly technical advice and support from a team of on-call experts. Technical support is provided from our web support page, and useful information can be obtained via our web-based forums (see below). There are no pricing policies after the 30 day money back guarantee period.

UK/International/
US Technical Support :   **http://www.serif.com/support**

Additional Serif contact information

Web:

Serif website: **http://www.serif.com**

Forums: **http://www.serif.com/forums.asp**

Main office (UK, Europe):

The Software Centre, PO Box 2000, Nottingham, NG11 7GW, UK

Main:	(0115) 914 2000
Registration (UK only):	(0800) 376 1989
Sales (UK only):	(0800) 376 7070
Customer Service (UK/International):	**http://www.serif.com/support**
General Fax:	(0115) 914 2020

North American office (US, Canada):

The Software Center, 17 Hampshire Drive, Suites 1 & 2, Hudson NH 03051, USA

Main:	(603) 889-8650
Registration:	(800) 794-6876
Sales:	(800) 489-6703
Customer Service:	**http://www.serif.com/support**
General Fax:	(603) 889-1127

International enquiries

Please contact our main office.

Introduction

Whether you are new to WebPlus or a seasoned website designer, the Resource Guide offers content to help you get the best out of WebPlus.

From a range of tutorials to get you started or help you accomplish a complex project, to full-colour previews of the navigation bars, colour schemes, gallery content, theme layouts, and pro templates, the Resource Guide is something you'll return to time and time again.

The Resource Guide is organized into the following chapters:

1: Tutorials

Illustrated, step-by-step training covering the basics of WebPlus and website design, along with some more projects on adding content to your website.

2: Navigation Bars

Previews of the customizable navigation bars included with WebPlus, and instructions on how to add them to your sites.

3: Colour Schemes

Previews of the professionally designed, customizable Colour Schemes included with WebPlus, and instructions on how to apply them.

4: WebPlus Gallery

Previews of the wide range of images included in WebPlus X5's Gallery tab, and instructions on how to add them to your sites.

5: Theme Layouts

Full-colour page previews of the theme layouts included on the WebPlus X5 Program DVD.

6: Pro Templates

A reference gallery of the design templates available on the WebPlus X5 Program DVD.

Contents

Chapter 1 - Tutorials   1

Accessing the Tutorials and Sample Files..3

Exploring WebPlus X5...5

Understanding Site Structure...7

Artistic Text..19

Frame Text..29

Creating Hyperlinks and Anchors...41

Pictures...59

Navigation Bars..81

Colour Schemes...93

Previewing and Publishing...105

Photo Galleries...117

Flash Objects..129

Panels I: Designing with Panels...135

Panels II: Assigning Actions...147

Contact Forms..159

E-Commerce...173

Chapter 2 - Navigation Bars   191

Chapter 3 - Colour Schemes   207

Chapter 4 - WebPlus Gallery   221

Chapter 5 - Theme Layouts   259

Chapter 6 - Pro Templates   303

Tutorials

Whether you are new to **Serif WebPlus X5** or an experienced user, these tutorials will help you to get the best out of the program.

As a new user, we recommend that you follow the tutorials in order as they will introduce you to the different concepts gradually. If you have used other Serif products, you'll find that many of the tools will already have a familiar feel.

Whatever your level of experience, you will be able to complete the tutorials if you follow the steps. Have fun!

Accessing the Tutorials

You can access the tutorials in one of the following ways:

- From the WebPlus Startup Wizard, select from the **Learn** section. Different icons indicate the type of tutorial available.

 a video tutorial

 an online tutorial

 see more tutorials and videos!

- or -

- From WebPlus, click **Help** and then click **Tutorials**.

Accessing the sample files

Throughout the tutorials, you'll be prompted to access sample files. All samples are accessible via the Internet at the following location:

http://go.serif.com/resources/WPX5

If you've clicked on a file, you can either open or save the file. We recommend you save the file to your desktop or a named folder on your computer.

Exploring WebPlus X5

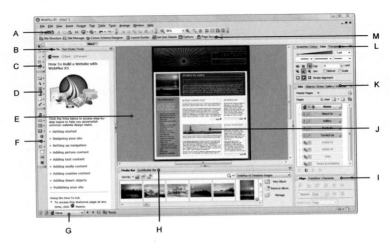

(**A**) Standard, Arrange and View toolbars, (**B**) How To, Text Styles, & Fonts tabs, (**C**) Tools toolbar, (**D**) Standard Objects toolbar, (**E**) Pasteboard area, (**F**) Web Objects toolbar, (**G**) Page Locator and Hintline toolbar, (**H**) Media Bar and QuickBuilder Bar, (**I**) Align, Transform, Character tabs, (**J**) Page area, (**K**) Site, Style, Gallery, Master Pages tabs, (**L**) Swatches, Colour, Line, Transparency tabs, (**M**) Context toolbar.

The WebPlus workspace

The WebPlus workspace consists of:

- A page area (**J**), where you put the text, graphics, and other elements that you want to appear on the final Web page.

- A surrounding pasteboard area (**E**), where you can keep elements that are being prepared or waiting to be positioned on the page area. (This is not displayed when the site is published.)

Understanding Site Structure

WebPlus provides simple, powerful tools that make it easy to design clearly structured websites that are easy to navigate. In this tutorial, we'll use a WebPlus template to introduce you to the basic elements of site structure.

By the end of this tutorial you will be able to:

- Create a new site from a template.

- Preview the site appearance.

- Navigate between pages.

- Create child pages.

- Change navigation preferences.

- Rearrange pages.

Let's begin...

1. On the **File** menu, click **Startup Wizard**.

2. In the Create section, click **Use Design Template**.

3. In the **Theme Layouts** category, select **Vintage**.

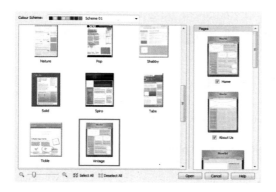

4. By default, all of the template pages are selected and the site uses Scheme 01. This is fine for our example so click **Open**.

    The 'Home' page is displayed in the workspace.

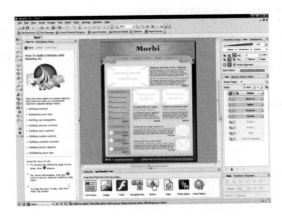

Creating websites with WebPlus X5

Creating a website in WebPlus can be as simple as choosing and customizing a design template, a theme layout (as in this example), or you can start from scratch. The building blocks that go on to make up your website are saved as a project file which will eventually be published to the Internet for all to see.

 Don't forget to save your work!

To save your work:

1. Before proceeding, click **File**, then **Save As...**

2. Save your project file with a file name of your choice.

Saving the WebPlus (.wpp) project file is not the same as publishing it as a website.

Understanding site structure

When you build your website, its important for you to have an understanding site structure and its hierarchy. We'll start by having a look at a preview of this site.

To preview your site:

1. On the toolbar at the top of the workspace, click the arrow on the  **Preview Site** button to expand a list of preview options.

2. Select **Preview Site in {your web browser of choice}**. WebPlus generates the necessary temporary files and opens a new browser window displaying the site's Home page.

The navigation bar (highlighted) interconnects the site's pages and is an indispensable element of site design. Users will expect it to be there, they'll know what to do with it, and it will help them grasp your site's main content sections at a glance.

Once you've experimented with the navigation bar, close the browser window and return to WebPlus. Now we'll have a look at the **Site** tab.

To navigate between pages:

1. At the right of the workspace, click the **Site** tab. This tab displays the
    Site Structure tree for this particular site. You'll recognize the
    entries as the main pages of the site.

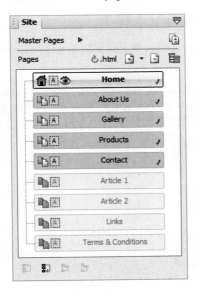

2. Double-click a page entry to open it in the workspace.

    As you change pages, notice that the  icon moves to indicate which
    page is currently in view and ready for editing.

3. In the lower left corner of the workspace, the Page Locator button shows the name of the current page. Click the button to display a list of the site's pages.

4. This time, single-click any page entry to view it.

   Watch the **Site** tab and you'll see the 👁 icon indicating the page on view.

5. If you single-click on a page in the tab, the page entry changes colour but the page is not displayed in the workspace. However, you can edit page properties and update other details.

Let's take a few moments to examine the site we created from the template.

Summary

• Single-click a page to select it—which you might do, for example, if you wanted to delete the page, or change its properties.

• Double-click a page to view it or edit its design elements.

The vertical order of the Web pages corresponds to the order in which they appear in the navigation bar. Page entries are connected by dotted lines, implying a certain relatedness.

Child pages

Let's now look at some different ways to get an overview of the entire site.

A parent-and-child 'tree' structure provides a natural framework for organizing site content into sections and levels. This site currently has one main page at the top level for each of our main sections. Over time we would expect to add subsidiary (child) pages to each section. Let's do this now.

To insert a child page:

1. On the **Site** tab, select the 'Gallery' page, and click the arrow on the ⬚ ˅ **Add** page drop-down list and select **New Blank Page...**

2. In the **New Page Properties** dialog:

   • On the **Navigation** option, in the **Page name:** text box, type 'Gallery 2'.

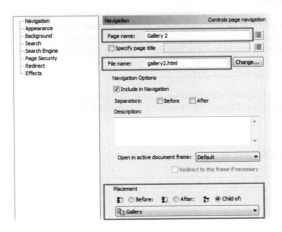

   • Change the **File name:** to 'gallery2.html'.

- In the **Placement** section, select the **Child of:** option.

- Click **OK**.

  A new page opens in the workspace, along with a new entry on the **Site** tab— which tells us the page title is 'Gallery 2' is currently on view (note the 👁 icon) but not selected.

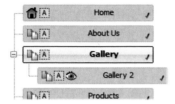

  More importantly, notice that the new 'Gallery 2' page entry is indented under 'Gallery'—in other words it's a child of 'Gallery', just as we specified in the dialog.

⭐ **Web page hierarchy**

Having inserted a new page in the 'Gallery' section of the site, we now have the makings of a hierarchy. Now the dotted lines connecting the page entries make more sense, and the Site Structure tree is no longer just a list.

⭐ If you add a new template page to your site, you will need to manually change this to be a child page. See the section *Page order* for more details.

⚠️ **Don't forget to save your work!**

Changing site navigation

If all of your pages were included in the site navigation, on a large website the navigation would be almost unusable. In WebPlus it's easy to specify whether or not a page is included.

On the **Site** tab, pages that are not included in the navigation (highlighted) are lighter in colour, and do not have a red check mark next to their names.

To change navigation options:

1. On the **Site** tab, right-click the 'Contact' page entry and click **Page Properties...**

2. In the **Page Properties** dialog, in the **Navigation** tab, clear the **Include in Navigation** check box and then click **OK**.

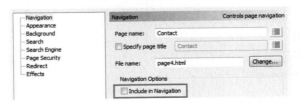

Notice what happens in the navigation bar:

Switching off the **Include in Navigation** setting for a page forces navigation bars to ignore that page, and its button disappears.

In the **Site** tab the 'Contact' page entry has changed colour and its red check mark is no longer displayed.

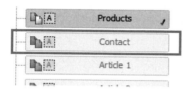

3. Open the **Page Properties** dialog again and select the **Include in Navigation** check box to reset it.

Page order

The buttons at the bottom of the **Site** tab also allow you to quickly and easily change pages from child to parent, or to move pages up or down in the list. To use any of these buttons, select the page that you want to move and then click the relevant button.

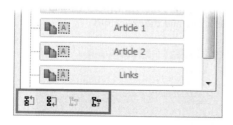

To change page order:

1. On the **Site** tab, click to select the 'Gallery' page.

2. Click the  **Move Page Up** button.

The page moves up the list while staying at the same hierarchy. Notice that the child pages are also moved as they are dependent on the parent page. As this page is included in the navigation, the navigation bar updates automatically to mirror the new top-level page order.

3. Experiment with the other pages and buttons.

Drag and Drop

You can change the order of the pages in the **Site** tab by dragging page entries to a different position. Watch the cursor change when you drag:

indicates that you can make the dropped page a child of the page above.

indicates that the page will land on the same level.

Most people grasp a branching structure fairly quickly, so organizing your content into a 'tree' structure helps your visitor navigate through it. As we've seen in this tutorial, the **Site** tab serves as a control centre that lets you, the designer, not only visualize your site's framework but manipulate it with ease.

You should now understand a little about site structure and how navigation bars adapt instantly to changes in the structure.

Artistic Text

When used correctly, Artistic text can enhance the visual impact of your website. It is generally reserved for use in logos, decorative headings, or situations where the text should stand out. Use Artistic text sparingly to keep your website looking professional and refreshing.

By the end of this tutorial you will be able to:

- Create and edit Artistic text.

- Resize text accurately.

- Apply and edit a gradient fill.

- Create a reflection effect.

- Create a second text object.

- Add an object to the Gallery.

Let's begin...

• On the **File** menu, click **New**.

    - or -

    In the Startup Wizard, in the Create section, click **Start New Site**.

A new blank document opens with a single page displayed in the **Site** tab.

Artistic Text

Now let's create a nameplate for a fictitious diving club, the Scuba Sharks. For this, we'll use artistic text...

To create artistic text:

1. On the Standard Objects toolbar, on the A ⏷ Text flyout, click the A **Artistic Text Tool**.

2. Click and drag anywhere on your page to set the size of your text.

    The Hintline toolbar tells us that this is Artistic Text and displays the size of the text. Set the text to approximately **78** pt.

3. On the Text context toolbar, in the Fonts drop-down list, select a bold font. We used Arial Black.

4. Type 'SCUBA'.

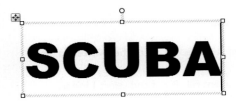

Now that our first word is placed, let's make it a little more interesting.

To accurately resize artistic text:

1. Click the text object border to select it. (The object border turns solid). On the **Transform** tab, ensure that the ▓ **Lock Aspect Ratio** is off. (If not, click the button once.)

2. Change the Width to **480 pix** and then change the Height to **120 pix**.

The text changes shape to fit the frame.

3. Click and drag the ⊕ **Move** button located just above the upper-left corner of the object (or click and drag on the object's border) to drag the object into position as illustrated.

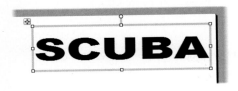

We can make the artistic text more interesting by adding a gradient fill.

To apply a gradient fill:

1. With the text object still selected, go to the **Swatches** tab.

2. Expand the  Gradient Fills flyout and select **Linear**.

3. Click the **Linear Fill 21** swatch to apply it to the text.

The gradient colour spread works well, but we can change the gradient to use scheme colours. This means that if we use the text in another document, it will tie in with any colour scheme.

To edit a gradient fill:

1. Select the text object and then on the Tools toolbar, on the Fill flyout, click the **Fill Tool**.

The object's fill path is displayed.

2. On the Fill context toolbar:

    *   In the **Fill Start** drop-down list, select swatch 6 on the Scheme 2 row.

- In the **Fill End** drop-down list, select swatch 8 on the Scheme 2 row.

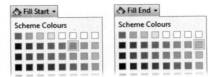

3. Click to select the right gradient fill path node. On the **Swatches** tab, set the **Tint** to 90%. (This adds more white to the scheme colour.)

4. (Optional) You can also adjust the fill path by clicking and dragging the fill path nodes.

The first part of our title is almost complete; however, let's make it look really special by adding a reflection effect.

To apply a reflection effect:

1. With the text object selected, go to the **Styles** tab and in the categories drop-down list, select **Reflection**.

2. In the **Artistic Text Reflections** sub-category, click the **Text Reflection 02 : FilterEffects** preset.

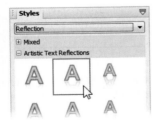

The reflection is applied.

To edit a reflection effect:

1. With the text object selected, on the Tools toolbar, in the ⬚ ▾ Effects flyout, click the ƒˣ **Filter Effects** button.

2. In the dialog:

    - If the preview is displayed, click **Show/Hide Preview** to hide the preview.

    - Drag the **Offset** slider to the left until the reflection sits just below the text. (The effect previews on the page.)

    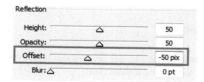

    - Click **OK**. The reflection is updated.

Next, we'll add our second word of our club name, 'SHARKS'. This time, we can use our existing object as a starting point.

Don't forget to save your work!

To create a second text object:

1. Select the SCUBA text object and click **Copy** then click **Paste**.

2. Click inside the new copy of the SCUBA text object and drag to select the letters 'CUBA'.

3. Type 'HARKS'. Notice that the formatting is retained.

4. Select the text object border and on the **Transform** tab, set the Width to **240 pix** and the Height to **55 pix**.

5. Finally, click and drag the ⊕ **Move** button to drag the object into position as illustrated.

To finish our club logo, we chose one of the designs from the **Gallery** tab **Logos** category and dragged it to the page.

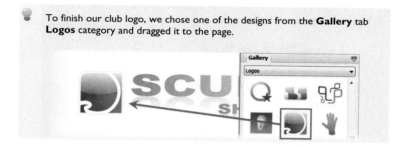

Now that we've created the club nameplate, we can add it to the gallery for use in other projects.

Don't forget to save your work!

To add objects to the Gallery:

1. Place the pointer in the workspace and then click and drag to select both objects with a selection marquee.

2. Click the  **Group** button.

3. On the **Gallery** tab, in the category drop-down list, select **My Designs**.

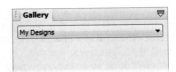

4. Press and hold the **Ctrl** key and drag a copy of the nameplate onto the **Gallery** tab.

5. In the dialog, type 'ScubaSharks' and click **OK**.

A copy of the object appears in the tab and is now ready for use in all of your future projects!

We added the gallery object to our scuba site. Notice because we used scheme colours, the design updates to match the current scheme.

There's a lot more that you can do with Artistic text, including putting it on various types of path, and adding instant 3D and other effects. The best way to learn is to experiment for yourself. If you get stuck, see the relevant topic in WebPlus Help. If you haven't done so already, you may want to have a look at the tutorial, *HTML frame text*.

Frame Text

To make your site as accessible as possible to everyone, you should use HTML text frames for your content. In this tutorial we look at the best ways of adding text to your website.

> ### WebPlus X5!
>
> Nulla vestibulum eleifend nulla. Suspendisse potenti. Aliquam turpis nisi, venenatis non, accumsan nec, imperdiet laoreet, lacus. In purus est, mattis eget, imperdiet nec, fermentum congue, tortor. Aenean ut nibh. Nullam hendrerit viverra dolor. Vestibulum fringilla, lectus id viverra malesuada, enim mi adipiscing ligula, et bibendum lacus...

By the end of this tutorial you will be able to:

- Create HTML text frames.

- Insert placeholder text.

- Select, edit and format text.

- Format text frames.

- Apply and edit Text Styles.

- Define HTML meta tags.

Let's begin...

- On the **File** menu, click **New**.

  - or -

  In the Startup Wizard, in the Create section, click **Start New Site**.

A new blank document opens with a single page displayed in the **Site** tab.

HTML frame text

There are three types of text in WebPlus—Artistic, Creative and HTML. Each type has different properties and they allow you to create great looking websites. However, any time you add effects such as bitmap fills, transparency, and filter effects to an artistic text object, the object is converted to a graphic when it is published. Similarly, in a Creative text frame, if you use an unusual font, or apply special formatting, the text will instead be rendered as a graphic. This can increase the download time of your website, and prevent the use of screen readers. To stop this from happening, all main body text content should ideally be placed inside an HTML text frame.

Let's start a new site so that we have a blank canvas.

 You'll see from the illustration above that the text colour looks different from our original design. This is because the document had a different colour scheme. When we applied the gradient fill, we used scheme colours. This means that the text will always use the current colour scheme. See the tutorial *Colour Schemes* on p. 93 or WebPlus Help for more information.

To place an HTML text frame:

1. On the Standard Objects toolbar, in the  Text Frames flyout, click the HTML Text Frame Tool.

2. Click and drag on the page to insert the frame at a size of your choice.

- or -

Click once on the page to insert the frame at its default size. (You can always resize it later.)

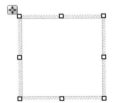

The HintLine toolbar tells you that this is an **HTML frame**.

Let's now fill our frame with some text. To save time when designing a site, you can fill any text frame (Creative or HTML) with placeholder text. This can help you (or your client) to visualise the overall design before the actual content is added.

To create placeholder text:

1. Click inside the text frame to create an insertion point, and then type the word 'Welcome'. Press **Return** to drop to the next line.

2. On the **Insert** menu, click **Fill with Placeholder Text**.

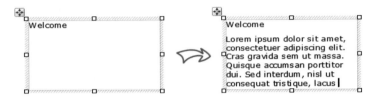

To select, edit and format text:

1. Click to place an insertion point after the word 'Welcome' and press the Spacebar. Type 'to ScubaSharks!'.

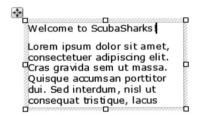

2. Triple-click (or click and drag) on the first line of text to select it.

3. On the Text context toolbar, in the styles drop-down list, select **Heading 1**. The heading is updated.

4. After step 3, you might find that the text no longer fits. You may also see an Overflow button.

This means that there is more text in the frame than can fit at one time. However, it's easy to resize a frame without changing the appearance of the text within. Let's do this now.

To resize a frame by dragging:

1. Move the mouser pointer over the frame's right-centre handle. The pointer will change to a double-headed arrow.

2. Click and drag to resize the frame so that it stretches across the page, leaving some extra space for additional text.

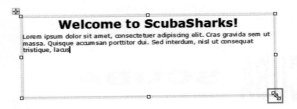

The actual text formatting doesn't change, it simply re-aligns to fit within the boundaries of the frame.

Let's add another heading to our text frame. This time, we'll format it using the **Heading 2** text style.

To format text using text styles:

1. Click inside the text frame to create an insertion point at the end of the existing text, and then press **Return** to drop to the next line. Type the words 'PADI Scuba courses'.

2. On the Text context toolbar, in the styles drop-down list, select **Heading 2**.

The style is applied to the text.

When you resize an HTML or Creative text frame, you are only resizing the text container. The formatting of the text will not change. However, resizing an Artistic text object once it is placed on the page will change the formatting of the text itself. Artistic text that is stretched or squashed will always be output as a graphic.

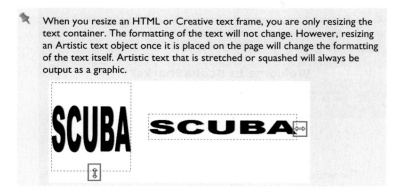

To select, copy and paste text:

1. Triple-click on the paragraph in the text frame. The entire paragraph is selected.

2. On the Standard toolbar, click **Copy** (or press **Ctrl + C**).

3. Click next to the word 'courses' and press **Enter** to create a new line.

4. Click **Paste** (or press **Ctrl + V**). The text is inserted.

 Changing the font

You can choose any font you like for your HTML text, but we recommend selecting from the **Fonts** tab's Websafe list for best possible results.

Don't forget to save your work!

Formatting Text Frames

If you want to make your text stand out from other text on your pages, why not format the text frame so that it creates an attractive container. Over the next few steps we'll apply a fill and padding to the text frame.

To change the fill colour of a text frame:

1. Click the text frame border to select the text frame (the border will turn to a solid outline).

2. On the Swatches tab, click the 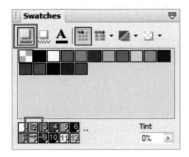 **Fill** button and then click a colour swatch to apply it. We selected Scheme Colour 2.

The fill is applied to your frame.

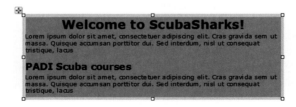

As you can see, the text goes right up to the edges of the frame. Now that we've added colour this doesn't look as good. We can improve things dramatically by adding some internal padding to the frame.

To add internal padding:

1. Ensure that the text frame is selected and on the Text context toolbar, click 📄 **Frame Setup**.

2. In the dialog, set the all four margins to 10 pix and click **OK**.

    The frame is updated.

3. (Optional) If necessary, resize the container to fit the text.

Text Styles

By using text styles, it makes it easy to keep the formatting of your text consistent.

We'll illustrate this by changing the text colour.

To update a text style:

1. (Optional) Click or hover over the | handle (near the Web Objects toolbar) to display the tabs on the left.

2. Click the **Text Styles** tab.

3. Move the mouse pointer over the **Normal** style and click the down-arrow. (If a style is not displayed, check **Show All** at the bottom of the **Text Styles** tab.)

4. Click **Modify Normal...**

5. In the **Text Style** dialog:

   • In the left pane, in the **Character** category, click the **Font** sub-category.

   • Click to expand the **Text colour** drop-down list and then click the Scheme Colour 11 swatch.

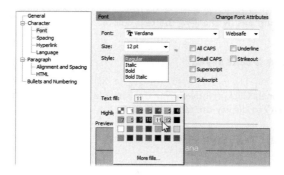

   • Click **OK**.

6. All of the body text in the frame is updated with the new colour!

By default, most styles are based on the **Normal** text style, so, by modifying Normal, the change is reflected throughout all of the Text Styles (and therefore your site). This makes it easy to quickly change the font, size and colour of your entire site.

Don't forget to save your work!

We couldn't finish this tutorial without looking at the main advantage of using HTML text frames—HTML meta tags. These are used by search engines to categorize your site. If you assign a meta tag to a text style, WebPlus will automatically generate the code when the site is published.

Let's do this now.

To apply an HTML meta tag to a style:

1. On the **Text Styles** tab, move the mouse pointer over the **Heading 1** style and click the down-arrow.

2. Click **Modify Heading 1...**

3. In the **Text Style** dialog:

   • In the left pane, in the **Paragraph** category, click the **HTML** sub-category.

- Select the appropriate HTML tag (in this case **H1** is already selected).

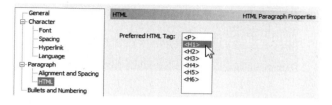

- Click **OK**.

The **H1** tag will be applied whenever the **Heading 1** style is used within an HTML text frame.

The **Text Styles** tab contains preset Heading styles which translate to HTML tags **H1** to **H6**. You can format the text style to suit your site design whilst keeping those important tags. For more information on modifying text styles see WebPlus Help.

We've covered many useful tips for creating, editing, and managing text with WebPlus. We hope that you're now feeling more comfortable with the different text objects we've described and are ready to get started creating content for your own site! If you haven't done so already, you may want to have a look at the tutorial, *Artistic text* on p.19.

Creating Hyperlinks and Anchors

WebPlus provides a wide and very flexible range of hyperlink options. This means easy navigation for your site's visitors—and possibly a more efficient visit if your site includes large pictures.

By the end of this tutorial you will be able to:

- Create anchors.

- Create a hyperlink to an anchor.

- Create a 'to top' hyperlink.

- Create self-linking picture hyperlinks.

- Create a link to a site page.

- Create external hyperlinks.

Go to **http://go.serif.com/resources/WPX5** to download the following tutorial project file(s):

  - **scuba.wpp**

Let's begin...

1.   On the Standard toolbar, click 📂 **Open**.

2.   Navigate to the **scuba.wpp** file, select it and click **Open**.

     The 'Home' page is displayed in the workspace.

🖫 **Save now!** Click **File > Save As...** and choose a new name for your file.

Introducing anchors and hyperlinks

Hyperlinks are an effective way of navigating around websites—when using the internet, you'll frequently use hyperlinks, perhaps even subconsciously.

Almost any object on your page can have a hyperlink assigned to it or can be the destination for a hyperlink. We'll explore the two most frequent examples—text and images.

We'll add some anchors and hyperlinks to the Scuba site.

We've added additional content to the **scuba.wpp** to help progress through this tutorial. If already completed, you may wish to use the website resulting from the tutorial *E-commerce* on p. 173.

Let's first look at setting up some page anchors.

Adding anchors

Anchors act as fixed points on your site which you can link to—anchors are used if you wish to direct visitors directly to a single point on a page rather than the entire page. Anchors must be created first before a hyperlink can established to it.

Let's imagine there is a sale on 'The Dive print' listed on the 'Shop' page. We want to highlight this fact on the 'Home' page and provide a direct link to the item on sale.

First we need to add an anchor to the sale item...

To add an anchor:

1.   On the **Site** tab, double-click the **Shop** page.

     The Shop page will be displayed in your workspace.

We've filled the empty picture frames with images from the **Media Bar** and placed frame text to the right of each image. For information on adding content, see the tutorials *Pictures* (p. 59) and *Frame Text* (p. 29).

2. Use the 🔺 **Pointer tool** to place an insertion point at the beginning the text box next to the bottom image—in our example, the words 'The Dive print'.

- or -

Use the 🔺 **Pointer tool** to select the bottom image.

We've also added sale stickers to the page using content from the **Gallery** tab. For more details on using the **Gallery** tab, see To add an object from the Gallery tab on p. 56.

3. On the **Insert** menu, and then click **Anchor**.

   - or -

   On the Tools toolbar, on the 🐾 ⁻ Hyperlink flyout, click 🔱 **Anchor.**

4. In the **Anchor** dialog box, type 'TheDiveSale,' and then click **OK**.
   (Note that anchor names cannot contain spaces.)

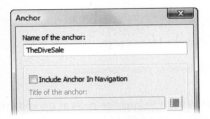

Anchors can be added to any object on any page, so it's possible to create unique navigation, and to offer speedy access to your site's content.

Anchors for important parts of your site can be included within site navigation maps or navigation bars by checking the **Include Anchor In Navigation** option. (In these cases, make sure that you give the anchor a meaningful title as this is what your site visitors will see.) For more information, see the tutorial *Navigation bars* on p. 81.

Linking to anchors

We now have an anchor which specifically identifies the sale item on the 'Shop' page. But how do we make use of this anchor?

To make the best use of an anchor, we need to create a hyperlink to take visitors to it!

To link to an anchor:

1. On the **Site** tab, double-click the **Home** page.

    The Home page will be displayed in your workspace.

2. Use the ⬉ **Pointer tool** to place an insertion point at the end main text frame. Press the **Return** key to create a new paragraph.

3. On the Frame text context toolbar, in the **Style** drop-down list, click **Heading 2**, and then click ☰ **Align Centre.**

4. Type 'Sale on selected prints!' and then drag with the ⬉ **Pointer tool** to select the text.

5. On the **Insert** menu, and then click **Hyperlink**.

    - or -

Click the arrow next to the **Anchor** tool to display the
Hyperlink flyout again, then click **Hyperlink** tool.

6. In the **Hyperlinks** dialog:

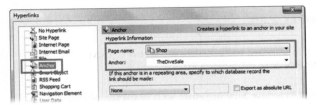

- Choose the **Anchor** option.

- In the **Page name** drop-down list, select **Shop**.

- In the **Anchor** drop-down list, select **TheDiveSale**.

- Click **OK**.

The **Export as absolute URL** option lets your site visitors add your page as a bookmark. This is especially important if you use frames to display content within your site.

The text now has a hyperlink attached to it.

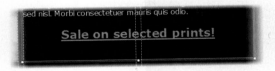

Don't forget to save your work!

Previewing your hyperlink

You now have a hyperlink to an anchor on a separate page, let's see how it works!

To preview a site:

1. On the Standard toolbar, click the arrow to expand the 🖥️ ▾ **Preview Site** drop-down list.

2. Select **Preview Site in {your web browser of choice}**.

3. Hover over the hyperlink and you will see the cursor change to the 🖑 hand cursor.

4. Click on the link and the 'Shop' page will display with 'The Dive print' in full view.

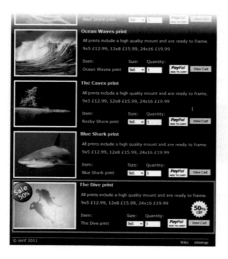

As you can see, the top of the page is not visible—this page is particularly long. Currently, to return to the top of the page, a visitor needs to scroll back up. Let's help our visitors by setting up a shortcut for returning to the top of the page.

Creating 'to top' hyperlinks

For long web pages you may want to offer a link back to the top of the page. You don't need to use an anchor to do this, just follow the steps below...

To create a 'top' link:

1. On the **Site** tab, double-click the **Shop** page.

   The Shop page will be displayed in your workspace.

2. On the Standard Objects toolbar, on the **A ·** Artistic Text flyout, click **A Artistic Text**.

3. Click at the bottom of the page to add a text object with default formatting.

4. Type 'Top of page' and then drag with the **✦ Pointer tool** to select the text.

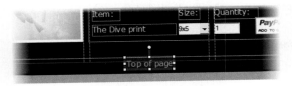

> ✦ You may wish to centre the text object on the page using the **Align** tab. For more information, see WebPlus Help.

5. On the **Insert** menu, and then click **Hyperlink**.

6. In the **Hyperlinks** dialog:

- Choose the **Anchor** option.

- In the **Anchor** drop-down list, select **top**.

- Click **OK**.

Feel free to preview your site, as mentioned on p. 48.

Don't forget to save your work!

Linking to pictures

We've just examined how to jump to specific points on a page, but hyperlinks can perform other tasks too. In the next section, we'll show you how to link to a larger version of a picture. This is useful if you want to show visitors a quick-loading, small thumbnail image but also allow them to access and download a larger, high resolution copy of the same image.

To create a 'self-linking' picture:

1. Use the **⬉ Pointer tool** to select an image—in our example, the 'Oceans Wave' image.

2. Right-click the image and click **Hyperlink...**

3. In the **Hyperlinks** dialog:

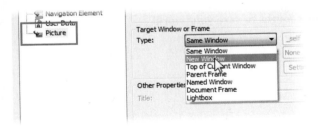

- Choose the **Picture** option.

- In the **Target Window or Frame** drop-down list, choose **New Window**.

- Click **OK**.

4. Feel free to preview your site, as mentioned on p. 48.

5. Go back to your project, right-click the image and choose **Properties.** You'll see that the thumbnail image is smaller compared to the original image.

When our site was published to a temporary folder for previewing purposes, WebPlus noticed that our resized 'thumbnail' was much smaller than the original image, so it created a much smaller version to make our page download more quickly. This is far more efficient and makes for a much faster page load!

 Don't forget to save your work!

Creating a link to a site page

Navigation bars are generally used for moving from one page to another within a website. However, there may be times when you have excluded pages from the main navigation bar but still want visitors to access them easily. A hyperlink can solve this problem. For more information, see the tutorial *Navigation bars* on p. 81.

In our scuba example, you can see that the 'Links' page has been excluded from the main navigation bar.

Let's create a hyperlink to the Links page and add a little flare by opening it in a lightbox.

To create a link to a site page:

1. On the **Site** tab, expand the **Master Pages** section, and then double-click on **Master A**.

    Master page A will display in the workspace.

    For more information on working with Master pages, see WebPlus Help.

2. Use the  **Pointer tool** to select the 'links' text in the bottom, right-hand corner of the page.

3. On the **Insert** menu, and then click **Hyperlink**.

4. In the **Hyperlinks** dialog:

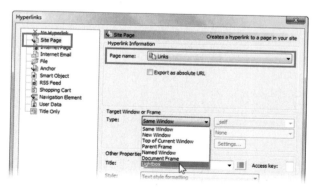

- Choose the **Site Page** option.

- Select **Links** from the **Page name** drop-down list.

- In the **Target Window or Frame** drop-down list, choose **Lightbox**.

- Click **OK**.

Feel free to preview your site, as mentioned on p. 48.

Don't forget to save your work!

Creating an external hyperlink

For this final section, we'll look at setting up a hyperlink on the 'About' page which links to an external website on the internet—such as Facebook or Twitter.

To add an object from the Gallery tab:

1. On the **Gallery** tab, from the category drop-down list, click **Icon Sets**.

2. From one of the sub-categories, click and drag a Facebook thumbnail onto your page.

Now we'll link it to Facebook—the procedure is very similar to previous explored throughout the tutorial.

To create an external hyperlink:

1. Right-click the object and then click Hyperlink....

2. In the Hyperlinks dialog:

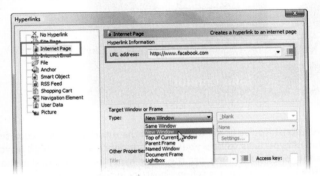

- Choose the **Internet Page** option.

- Type in the URL for the external site in the **URL address** box or click a previously entered URL from the drop-down list.

- In the **Target Window or Frame** drop-down list, choose **New Window**.

- Click **OK**.

 Whenever linking to an external website, we recommend setting the target window or frame to **New Window**, this way your visitor will not lose access to your website—it will still be open in their browser.

Feel free to preview your site, as mentioned on p. 48.

Congratulations! You've come to the end of the tutorial and the scuba site is now full of hyperlinks to help your visitors navigate around. We'll leave you to add more links and explore the other hyperlink types listed in the **Hyperlinks** dialog—most are self-explanatory in their nature.

Hyperlinks and anchors can be viewed and managed from the **Site Manager**, which you can access from the context toolbar.

For more information on using **Site Manager**, see WebPlus Help.

Pictures

Using pictures is a great way to create an eye-catching website. However, used incorrectly, they can slow the loading of your site and frustrate visitors. WebPlus has a few tricks for placing images while optimizing page download. We'll introduce you to these tricks for importing, placing, and managing images on your website.

By the end of this tutorial you will be able to:

- Use picture frames.

- Adjust pictures in frames.

- Use the **Media Bar**.

- Import and place images on the page.

- Create self-linking picture hyperlinks.

- Apply various image effects.

- Modify global and individual image format settings.

- Add ALT and TITLE text to pictures.

Let's begin...

1. On the **File** menu, click **Startup Wizard**.

2. In the Create section, click **Use Design Template**.

3. In the dialog:

   • In the **Theme Layouts** list on the left, select the **Vintage** sub-category.

   • In the right **Pages** pane, select **Home** only.

4. Click **OK**.

   The layout opens in the workspace.

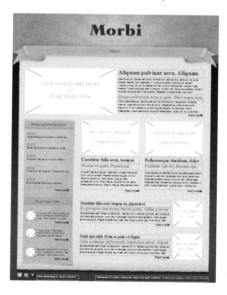

This theme layout page provides several 'placeholder' picture frames for you to add your own photos.

Using picture frames

Placing picture frames on your site pages has several benefits:

- You can use empty frames as 'placeholder' areas when you know you want to add images, but have yet to put them in, as in WebPlus theme layouts.

- Frames make it easy to place images at a specific size or shape, without changing the aspect ratio—useful for 'contact' pictures or thumbnails.

- You can easily swap the images displayed inside frames without altering the page layout in any way.

You can add pictures individually by clicking directly on a placeholder, or you can add multiple pictures to the **Media Bar** and then drag them onto the frames as you need them. We'll demonstrate both methods. We'll be using the sample images installed with WebPlus. However, you can use your own images if you prefer.

To add a picture to a frame:

1. Select the large picture frame and then click 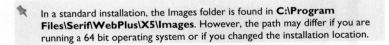 **Replace Picture**.

    - or -

    Double-click inside the large picture frame.

2. In the **Import Picture** dialog, browse to your **Images** folder.

> In a standard installation, the Images folder is found in **C:\Program Files\Serif\WebPlus\X5\Images**. However, the path may differ if you are running a 64 bit operating system or if you changed the installation location.

3. Select the blue car picture (2703912.jpg) and click **Open**.

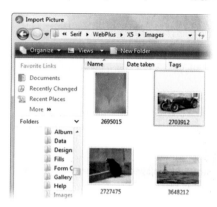

4. The picture is added to the frame and scaled to maximum-fit by default.

When the picture is selected, note that the **Picture Frame** toolbar displays in the lower-right corner. You can use these tools to adjust your picture inside the frame.

To adjust a picture inside a frame:

- To reposition the picture inside the frame, click  **Pan**, and then click and drag on the picture with the 🖐 **Pan** cursor.

- To rotate the picture counter-clockwise, in 90° increments, click ⬆ **Rotate**.

- To zoom in or out of the picture, click 🔍 **Zoom In** or 🔍 **Zoom Out**, and then click on the picture.

- To replace the picture, click 🖼 **Replace Picture**, browse to and select a new picture and click **Open**.

- To change the scale options, on the Picture context toolbar, click 🖼 **Frame Properties** and change the option in the dialog.

Using the Media Bar

WebPlus provides a wealth of royalty-free pictures for you to use in your website. These are conveniently stored in the Media Bar for easy access and quick addition to your site. These images are organized into various albums available from the album drop-down list in the Media Bar.

 Viewing the Media Bar
If you can't see the **Media Bar**, click the ▬▬ handle at the bottom of the workspace.

We've provided a convenient **Tutorial Images** album which contains all the images you will need to help you progress through WebPlus tutorials.

To add a picture to a frame using the Media Bar:

1. On the **Media Bar**, in the rightmost drop-down list, select the **WebPlus X5 - Tutorial Images** album.

2. Drag the photo of the train (train_06.jpg) onto a picture frame.

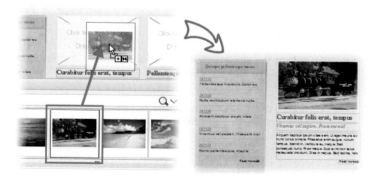

You might prefer to add your own pictures to the **Media Bar** before adding them to your site.

To add images to the Media Bar:

1. By default, the **Media Bar**, displays a **Temporary Album**. If not, select this in the rightmost drop-down list.

2. Click in the blank area of the tab.

   - or -

   Click 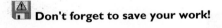 **Add Image**.

   In the **Import Picture** dialog, navigate to the folder where you keep your images.

3. Select your files and click **Open**. The photos are displayed as thumbnails on the **Media Bar**.

You can always save your temporary album to use in other sites. Click 🖼 **Add To** and then click **New Album**.

🔔 **Don't forget to save your work!**

Adding picture frames

If you're developing a site from scratch you may wish to add picture frames to your page for the reasons highlighted above. Let's do that now...

- On the **File** menu, click **New**.

  - or -

  In the Startup Wizard, in the Create section, click **Start New Site**.

A new blank document opens with a single page displayed in the **Site** tab.

To add a picture frame:

1. On the Standard Objects toolbar, on the 🖾 ▾ Picture flyout, click ⊠ **Empty Picture Frame**.

2. Click and drag to create a rectangular frame.

   - or -

   Shift-click and drag to create a square frame.

Adding pictures directly to a page

Although picture frames can be useful in building and updating a site, you can also add pictures directly to a page, without using picture frames.

You can add pictures individually by using the **Import Picture** tool, or you can add multiple pictures to the **Media Bar** and then drag them onto your page as you need them. We'll demonstrate both methods. We'll be using the sample images installed with WebPlus. However, you can use your own images if you prefer.

To import an image:

1. Click on the empty picture frame and then press **Delete**.

2. On the Standard Objects toolbar, on the ▨ ▾ Picture flyout, click ▨ **Import Picture**.

3. In the **Import Picture** dialog, browse to your **Images** folder.

4. Select the blue car picture (2703912.jpg) and click **Open**.

5. Your cursor changes to the ▪◾ Picture Import cursor.

    Click and drag on the page to create a small 'thumbnail' version of the image.

💡 You can scale an image at any time by selecting it and dragging its handles.

To add images using the Media Bar:

1. On the **Media Bar**, in the rightmost drop-down list, select the **WebPlus X5 - Tutorial Images** album.

2. Drag the photo of the blue car (2703912.jpg) onto the page.

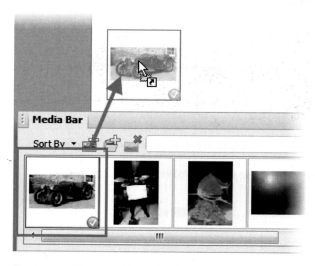

The image will open at its native size.

Previewing images

Your page should now contain two identical images with different
dimensions.

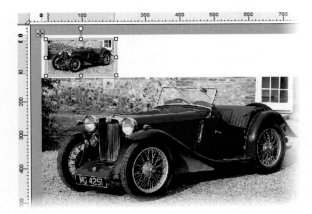

Previewing images in an internet browser window allows you to get an
idea of how they will appear when published. It will also give you an
indication of the file size of the published image.

To preview published image size:

1. On the Standard toolbar, click the arrow to expand the
    Preview Site drop-down list.

2. Click the **Preview in Window (Internet Explorer)** option.

    Once exported, WebPlus displays the site preview in a built-in
    Microsoft Internet Explorer window.

3. Right-click each image in turn and click **Image Properties**.

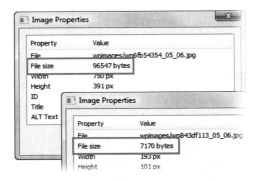

Notice that the smaller image also has a smaller file size. (Note also that the files are no longer called **2703912.jpg**. This is because WebPlus has created new versions of the image.)

Both pictures use the same source image, but WebPlus has downsampled the smaller version to recreate it using fewer pixels, so your page will download more quickly.

4. Click ⊠ **Close Preview** to return to the WebPlus workspace.

Upsampling and downsampling

The terms **downsampling** and **upsampling** are used to describe the recreation of images with either fewer or more pixels respectively.

An upsampled image has more pixels than the original, and can be done in image editing software such as **Serif PhotoPlus**. The additional pixels are added by clever mathematical guesswork. Upsampled images often have a larger file size than the original image.

A downsampled image has fewer pixels than the original, and therefore, a smaller file size, When an image has been reduced in size on the page, WebPlus generally downsamples automatically at publication time, outputting a reduced-resolution image that fits the space allocated to it on the page.

Linking from a thumbnail to a larger image

Suppose you want your site's visitors to be able to view high-resolution images while keeping the page size small. Here's an excellent approach:

To create a self-linking hyperlink:

1. Click on the large image to select it and then press **Delete**.

2. Select the small image and reposition it towards the top of the page.

3. With the image still selected, on the Tools toolbar, on the 🔍 ▾ Hyperlink flyout, click 🔍 **Hyperlink**.

4. In the **Hyperlinks** dialog, select the **Picture** option.

   In the **Target Window or Frame** section select **Lightbox** from the **Type** drop-down list.

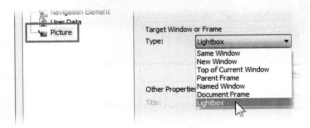

   Click **OK**.

5. In the **HTML Preview** drop-down list, click **Preview in {your web browser of choice}**.

Hover the mouse over the image—the cursor changes to a hand.

Click to see a full-size version of the image displayed in a lightbox.

For more information on using lightboxes, see WebPlus Help.

6. Close the browser preview when you have finished experimenting.

This 'self-linking picture' hyperlink method is a favoured way of offering images to your site's visitors—the smaller image is quick to download, providing faster-loading pages, and only the visitors who want to see the full size image need to download it. This eliminates unnecessary bandwidth usage.

 Don't forget to save your work!

Applying adjustments and effects

Now let's move on and discuss a few more hints and tips for enhancing your pictures...

To add transparency effects:

1. With the image selected, click the **Transparency** tab and expand the **Bitmap** drop-down list.

2. Click to display the **Photo Edge Effects** category and then click the **Bitmap Transparency 10** swatch.

3. Click to expand the **HTML Preview** drop-down list and click **Preview in Window**.

    Let's now see how these changes have affected the way in which WebPlus publishes the image.

4. In your browser, right-click on the image and choose **Image Properties**.

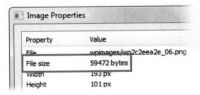

Note the image size (59472 bytes in our case). This is different to the reported size of our original thumbnail image, placed in step 2 (7170 bytes).

The use of transparency on our image means that WebPlus must achieve the effect by creating and publishing a modified version of our image.

Other effects and operations that will cause recreation of an image include: cropping, rotation, most filter effects, recolouring, and significant overlaps of other objects.

5. Click ⊠ **Close Preview** to return to the WebPlus workspace.

To recolour an image:

1. Select the image and click the 🖼 **Re-colour Picture** button on the Picture context toolbar.

2. In the **Fill** dialog, click a black colour swatch and then click **OK**.

3. Try experimenting with other colours, for example, create a sepia tone effect by applying a brown or dark orange fill colour.

This creates an 'old photo' effect and can work well with the Photo Edge Effects used in the previous section.

To apply an image adjustment:

- With the image selected, on the Picture context toolbar, click **⟳** **Increase Contrast**. Repeat as required.

- (Optional) Experiment with the other adjustments provided on the Picture context toolbar to see how they affect your images.

🔖 **Advanced image adjustments**

WebPlus includes a powerful mix of advanced image correction and adjustment tools— including levels, colour balance, channel mixer, HSL, and Unsharp Mask—and a selection of creative effects such as Diffuse Glow and Gaussian Blur. All of these are applied from the **PhotoLab** dialog, which you can open by clicking **PhotoLab** on the Picture context toolbar.

For more information, see WebPlus Help.

💾 **Don't forget to save your work!**

Image formats

Finally, we'll discuss another consideration when importing images and using drawn objects or 'fancy' text—**image formats**.

Imported images can have a variety of image formats (WebPlus supports the import of many different image formats), but most current Web browsers can only display **GIFs**, **JPGs**, and **PNGs**.

Image compression formats

PNG is a 'lossless' compression format that generally produces very small files. In its 32-bit format, it supports a transparent alpha channel. The PNG format is ideal for images containing text, line-art. graphics and solid blocks of colour, or small images containing gradients. However, it is extremely inefficient for photographic and photo-like images.

JPEG/JPG files have a 'lossy' compression format, that supports both RGB and CMYK colour spaces. JPEG compression is specifically designed for photos as it produces the smallest file size and highest for this type of image.

GIF compression produces very small files. It supports a simple, single level of transparency (each pixel is either on or off). The file format is restricted by only supporting 256 colours. GIFs can also be animated.

For more information on the various file types, see WebPlus Help.

Images imported in one of these three Web-friendly formats may be published in their original format, untouched by WebPlus's intelligent image converter.

When necessary, WebPlus converts objects and images into a suitable format.

However, for drawn objects, modified artistic text, and imported images, you can set the individual or global image conversion options for your preferred published results.

Let's see how you can modify both global and individual image export settings, starting with global settings.

To set global image export options:

1.   On the **File** menu, click **Site Properties**.

In the **Site Properties** dialog, the **Graphics** option offers global options for handling graphics when publishing your site.

By default:

- Generated graphics (drawn objects, text with non-solid fills, objects with transparency or filter effects, or cropped/rotated objects) will be exported as PNG for best quality.

- JPGs will be exported as JPGs, even when resampled (you can adjust the compression for resampled JPGs).

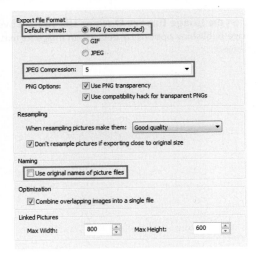

Note that when the original file is used, it will be renamed unless you select the **Use original names of graphic files** check box.

2.   Click **OK** to close the **Site Properties** dialog.

For the ultimate in finding the right balance between file size and image quality for your site's images, consider exporting them from a program that offers a full **Export Optimizer** with export quality and file size preview, such as Serif PhotoPlus.

If you have PhotoPlus 10 or later installed, click the ⚫ **Edit in PhotoPlus** button on the Picture context toolbar to open the image for editing.

You can also override the default settings for particular images. This can be useful when you want a specific format to be output.

To set individual export options:

1. Right-click on a picture and choose **Export Options...**.

2. In the dialog, on the **Image Export Options** tab, you can override the global image publishing options by defining an image format for the selected object.

ALT & TITLE text

ALT and TITLE text is important to use to ensure that your website is accessible to everyone.

- TITLE text is the tooltip text that will appear when site visitors hover over the image in their Web browsers. This text is often used when clicking on a image has some function, for example, opening a larger version of the image in a new window.

- ALT text, used to describe the content and/or purpose of an image, is the text that will appear in the area of your page where the image will download. (Note that ALT text should *not* be used for images whose only purpose is decorative.)

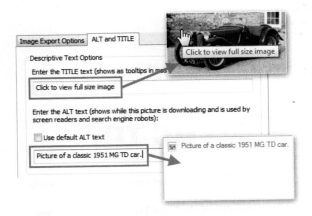

To set ALT and TITLE text for an image:

1. Right-click on a picture and choose **Export Options...**.

2. In the dialog, on the **ALT and TITLE** tab, enter pop-up TITLE and ALT text.

By default, the **Use default ALT text** option is selected. This tells WebPlus to use the TITLE text as the ALT description so that you only have to enter it once. By clearing the check box (as we have done) you can have different ALT and TITLE text. You can also choose to only have ALT text.

In order to accurately reproduce your design as a Web page, it is possible that items you create in WebPlus will be published as images. To allow for this, ALT and TITLE options are available for regular WebPlus objects as well as for imported images.

WebPlus will attempt to create ALT text for any text that is exported as a graphic.

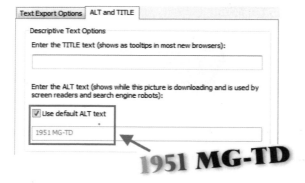

For more information, see *Setting Picture Export Options* in WebPlus Help.

We suggest that you experiment with ALT and TITLE text and preview your results. ALT text is an important consideration when making your site accessible to as many people as possible, and it may even help improve your site's rankings in search engine results.

In this tutorial, we've explored some image import options, some efficiency and quality issues, and some publishing considerations.

For more information, see the tutorial *Hyperlinks* (p. 41).

Navigation Bars

Having fantastic content on your website is useless unless your visitors can get to it! Navigation bars are essential to successful site navigation. Luckily for us, WebPlus has a whole host of professionally designed dynamic navigation bars for us to use, and the process is easy.

By the end of this tutorial you will be able to:

- Change the design of an existing navigation bar.

- Customize a navigation bar.

- Use Child and Same Level navigation bars.

- Insert a site map.

> If you're unfamiliar with website structure, we suggest you review the basic concepts before beginning this tutorial. See WebPlus Help or the *Site Structure* tutorial on p.5.

Let's begin...

1. On the **File** menu, click **Startup Wizard**.

2. In the Create section, click **Use Design Template**.

3. In the dialog:

    - In the **Theme Layouts** list on the left, click **Doodle**.

    - Click **OK**.

        The page opens in the workspace.

Changing the style of an existing navigation bar

Notice that this template already contains a navigation bar.

Generally, the main **'top level'** navigation bar is shared by all of the pages on a website. As a result, the navigation bar is usually placed on the underlying master page. This means that you only have to place the navigation bar once, even though it appears on each page. The bar on this layout is very small so let's update it to something a little different.

To change the navigation bar design:

1. Click to select the existing navigation bar and then click 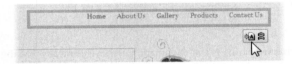 **Edit on Master Page**.

The master page is displayed in the workspace.

2. Double-click the navigation bar to open the **Navigation Bar Settings** dialog.

3. In the dialog, click to display the **Type** tab.

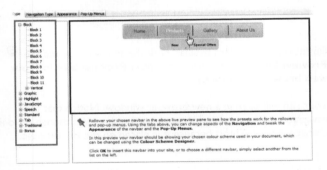

The category list (highlighted red) displays the available navigation bar categories. A preview is displayed in the main pane (highlighted blue). Click on a category item to view a preview of the bar. (If you point to a part of the bar containing a pop-up menu the menu will also preview.) We selected the Block 9 navigation bar style.

4. For now we'll accept the default appearance. Click **OK** to exit.

   The navigation bar is updated on the page.

   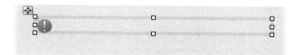

   Notice that we have a green exclamation mark. This means that the bounding box is too small for our navigation bar to fit into.

5. Drag on the bounding box handles until the navigation bar can fit inside. The green exclamation mark will disappear when all of the navigation bar can display correctly.

6. Finally, on the Standard toolbar, click the arrow to expand the 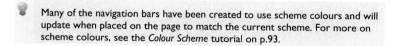 **Preview Site** drop-down list and select **Preview Site in {your web browser of choice}**.

   Your site will open in a new browser window. Notice that the navigation bar has updated throughout the site, even though we only changed it once, This is because it is placed on the master page.

💡 Many of the navigation bars have been created to use scheme colours and will update when placed on the page to match the current scheme. For more on scheme colours, see the *Colour Scheme* tutorial on p.93.

Customizing a navigation bar

Now let's customize one of the pre-designed navigation bars.

 The **scuba.wpp** example file that is used throughout the tutorials uses a standard navigation bar from the **Block** category, that has been customized to use the site's scheme colours.

To customize the navigation buttons:

1. Double-click the navigation bar to open the **Navigation Bar Settings** dialog.

2. Click to display the **Appearance** tab. Notice that a dynamic preview of the navigation bar displays at the bottom of the dialog.

Here you can change the style of the buttons, separators and background. You can even create your own design from scratch! This would be a tutorial in itself, so for now, we'll just change the style of the buttons to one of the pre-designed ones.

3. Click the arrow next to the **Single:** button. A drop-down list of all
    available buttons is displayed. Click to select a different button. We
    decided on one of the buttons in the **Traditional** category.

The preview updates to show your new button in place.

4. To preview your navigation bar on a different 'page' background
    colour, select a different swatch from the **Preview Background:**
    drop-down palette. This will help you to decide whether your
    navigation bar will fit in with you site background.

5. When you're happy with your changes, click **OK**.

6. Click **Preview Site in {your browser of choice}** to see your new
    navigation bar in action.

Buttons, backgrounds and separators are created using images with special properties.

If you want to be more adventurous with your navigation bar or button design, click on the ✎ Edit button. This will take you into the appropriate design studio. You'll find detailed information on using the design tools in the studio **How To** pane.

Other types of navigation

In most websites, the main navigation bar is kept fairly simple, showing only the main, top-level pages of the website. However, it is not uncommon to have several types of navigation bar used throughout your website. WebPlus makes this process very easy—it is even possible to maintain a consistent look throughout by sharing navigation bar styles between navigation bars. We don't have time to go into that now, but you can find out more about this in WebPlus Help.

We'll conclude this tutorial by looking at a few examples from a completed version of our scuba website. However, we won't go into step-by-step detail—the general formatting process is much the same as the steps we followed to create our top-level navigation earlier in the tutorial.

If you want to look at our examples in action, you'll need a copy of the **scuba.wpp** file. If you haven't already downloaded it, you can do so now.

 Go to **http://go.serif.com/resources/WPX5** to download the following tutorial project file(s):
  ◉ **scuba.wpp**

Same Level navigation bar

Each of the diver's personal pages has a **Same Level** navigation bar. This makes it easy for the visitor to jump between these child pages, without having to use the drop-down list off the main navigation bar. It also makes it obvious at a glance that there is more to explore.

The bar itself has been added as a single object to a new **Master B** page which is assigned to the child pages in addition to the main master page, **Master B**.

You can assign multiple master pages in the Site tab by simply dragging additional master pages onto the page entry. A ⊞ is displayed on the entry to signify that it now uses more than one master page.

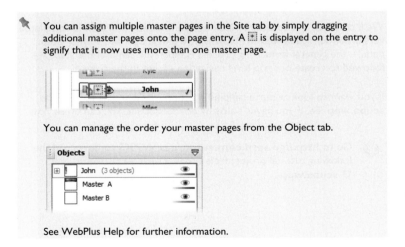

You can manage the order your master pages from the Object tab.

See WebPlus Help for further information.

To add a Same Level navigation element:

1. Ensure that the page to which you want to add the navigation bar (Master B in our example **scuba.wpp** file) is displayed in the workspace.

2. Drag the **Navigation Bar** element from the **QuickBuilder Bar** (at the bottom of the workspace) to your page.

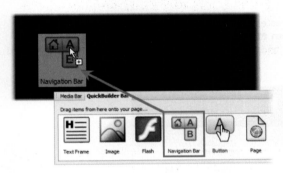

3. The **Navigation Bar Settings** dialog opens:

   - Choose a navigation bar design from one of the categories.

   - On the **Navigation Type** tab, click **Same Level**.

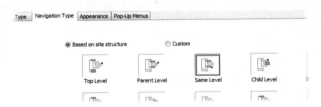

   - If required you can modify appearance and pop-up menus in the relevant tabs.

4. Click **OK** to accept changes and exit the dialog.

Child Level navigation bar

On our website we have a **Top Level**, 'About Us' page which contains three child pages. We wanted a navigation bar to display child pages only. To keep the navigation consistent, we used the navigation bar on the **Master B** page. However, this caused the navigation to show the wrong pages as it was set to **Same Level** navigation, we needed to change it to **Child Level**.

Rather than create an entire new master page, we simply use the **Promote from Master Page** to create a special instance of the navigation bar, and then change the navigation settings to display **Child Level** pages.

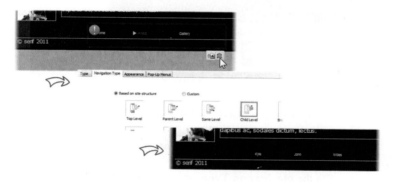

This form of navigation allows the visitor to get to relevant pages on the site, without delving through menus. It also makes it plainly obvious that there is more content to see.

Site maps

Our final navigation example is a site map. This is a special type of navigation element that displays every page in your site. It allows visitors to jump straight to any page and can help to elevate your site's status within search engines.

Normally, a site map is placed on a page that is not included within any of the navigation bars. (This is shown by a grey page entry in the **Site** tab.) Instead, a simple link is provided to it on the master page. However, smaller sites may place a sitemap at the bottom of a master page.

To add a Site Map navigation element:

1. In the **Site** tab, double click on the 'Sitemap' page to display it in the workspace.

2. At the bottom of the workspace drag the **Navigation Bar** element from the **QuickBuilder Bar** to your page.

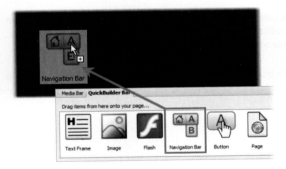

3. The **Navigation Bar Settings** dialog opens:

    •   In the left-most category list, choose **Javascript > Site Map**. The navigation element is displayed in the preview pane. Select one of the available designs.

- On the **Navigation Type** tab, ensure that the **Include anchors** check box is selected if you have used anchors in your site.

- If required you can set advanced options and change the appearance in the **Options** and **Style** tabs.

4. When you're finished, click **OK**. The sitemap is placed on the page.

Well, that concludes this tutorial. We hope this exercise has convinced you of the versatility of navigation bars that not only adapt to your site structure but blend harmoniously with your site's visual design.

Equipped with a basic knowledge of these remarkable WebPlus features, you're ready to create your own website layouts. Now it's up to you and your imagination!

Colour Schemes

When designing your publications, one of the most important factors to consider is colour. It sets the mood, sends a message and gets attention. But how do you select a colour palette that's right for your publication? In the first of the colour schemes tutorials, we'll introduce you to WebPlus colour schemes.

In the first section of this tutorial, we'll apply scheme colours to individual elements on a page. We'll then show you how you can edit and modify scheme colours.

By the end of this tutorial you will be able to:

- Apply a preset colour scheme.

- Apply a scheme colour to objects.

- Modify an existing colour scheme.

- Save a modified scheme.

Let's begin...

1. On the **File** menu, click **Startup Wizard**.

2. In the Create section, click **Use Design Template**.

3. In the dialog:

   • In the **Theme Layouts** list on the left, click **Doodle**.

   • Click **OK**.

   The page opens in the workspace.

Changing the scheme colour

This site has been designed to use colour schemes. Let's look at this now by choosing a different scheme.

To apply a colour scheme:

1. On the **Swatches** tab click the ·· button (next to the colour swatches).

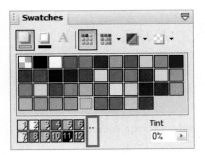

The Colour Scheme Designer opens. In the Scheme Manager pane, you'll see an assortment of named schemes, each consisting of twelve basic colours. The colour scheme that is currently applied is highlighted in the **Scheme Manager** pane and displayed on the right.

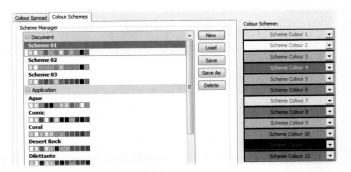

2. On the **Colour Schemes** tab, click to select **Scheme 2** and then click **Load**.

All schemed objects within the publication update with the new colours.

3. Select **Scheme 3**, click **Load** and click **OK** to exit the dialog.

 If you take a look at our pro design templates, you'll notice that these are also designed to use colour schemes so that you can change the look and feel quickly and easily.

Applying scheme colours to objects

The scheme colours work much like a paint-by-numbers system, where various regions and elements of a page layout are coded with numbers. In each scheme, a specific colour is assigned to each number. You can change or even apply a colour scheme at any point during the design process, but it's best practice to scheme your objects from the start. This gives you the most flexibility if you decide to change the look and feel of a publication.

 A publication can only have one colour scheme in use at any given time.

To apply a scheme colour to an object:

1. On the Tools toolbar, on the QuickShape flyout, click the ☆ **Quick Petal** and draw a large shape on the page.

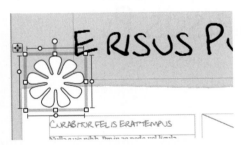

2. Click to display the **Swatches** tab.

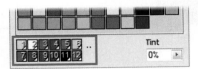

   At the bottom of the tab, below the colour swatches, you'll see that twelve scheme colours appear as numbered swatches.

3. Ensure that the shape is selected and on the **Swatches** tab, click the
    Fill button and then click the scheme colour you want to apply to
    the shape's fill.

4. Now apply a different colour scheme to the publication. WebPlus
    applies the new scheme colours to the shape.

On the **Swatches** tab, notice that the colour scheme swatches have
been replaced with the new scheme colours.

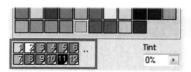

You can also apply scheme colours to text in the same way.

As you can see, when you create new elements in any publication, you can extend a colour scheme to your layout elements using the process just described.

 If you copy an object that uses scheme colours to another WebPlus publication, the object will take on the colour scheme used in the new document.

You'll need to spend some time working out which colour combinations look best, but the mechanics of the process are simple.

 Don't forget to save your work!

Modifying colour schemes

If you've tried various colour schemes but haven't found one that's quite right for your document, you can modify any of the colours in an existing scheme to create a new one.

To modify a colour scheme:

1. On the **Swatches** tab click the ·· button (next to the colour swatches).

    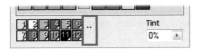

2. In the **Colour Scheme Designer** dialog, the current scheme colours are displayed.

    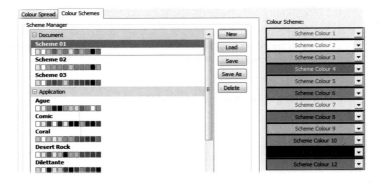

    Each of the twelve scheme colours has its own drop-down list, showing available colours.

3. To set or change a scheme colour, simply click the button to expand the drop-down list, and then select a new colour.

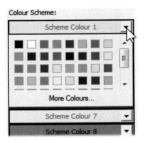

4. (Optional) If the drop-down palette doesn't contain the colour you want to use, click **More Colours** to display the **Colour Selector**.

    In the **Colour Selector** dialog, various controls allow you to choose a colour to apply or mix your own custom colours.

    - You can either drag on the colour space (red highlight) or use the ✎ **Colour Picker** (blue highlight) to pick up a colour from anywhere.

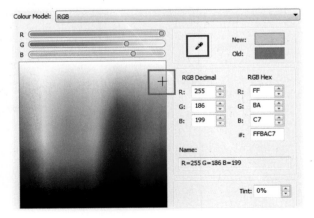

- To see a list of colours associated with the current publication, choose **Palette** from the **Colour Model** drop-down list.

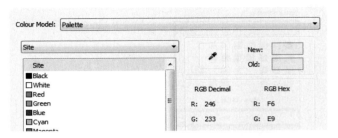

- Click **OK** to save changes and exit the dialog.

5. When you have modified your scheme, click **OK** to apply it to your publication.

To preview your site in a Web browser:

1. Click the arrow to expand the 🖥▾ **Preview Site** drop-down list.

2. Select **Preview Site in {your web browser of choice}**.

3. Your site will open in a new browser window.

> If you have installed a browser that does not appear in the Preview List, you may need to add it manually. For more information see *Previewing your website* in WebPlus Help.

> As of early 2011, the most popular browsers are Firefox, Internet Explorer and Google Chrome respectively, however, they behave differently so it's important to see how your site appears in each of them. Other browsers such as Opera (especially for mobile devices) and Safari are also supported by WebPlus. Browsers can be freely downloaded and it's worth installing a few different ones.

Publishing

We'll assume that our design looks great in a range of browsers. Now it's time to publish our site to a live location. Even though you may have saved your website as a WebPlus project, it's not truly a 'website' until you've converted it to files that can be viewed in a Web browser. WebPlus does this automatically when you publish the site.

Publishing options

WebPlus can publish your site in several ways:

*   **Publish to a Disk Folder** - lets you use your site as a network-based Intranet, write it to CD-ROM for distribution, or upload it manually to an Internet server using file transfer protocol (FTP) software.

*   **Publish to the Web** - publish your page or site directly to a Web server so that it can be viewed over the Internet.

*   **Quick Publish to Web** - publish only the page that you are currently working on directly to the Web server.

> ⚠ **Note:** The next steps assume that you have dedicated space on a web server. If you are unsure how to access this, contact your service provider.

To publish to the Web:

1. Check your page names, file names, and picture export settings in the **File > Site Properties...** and **Format > Image Export Options...** dialogs. (For details, see WebPlus Help.)

2. In 🖼 **Site Manager** (on the Default context toolbar), use **Site Checker** to check your site for problems such as non-websafe fonts, invalid anchors and hyperlinks, and so on. (See WebPlus Help for more details.)

3. On the Standard toolbar, click 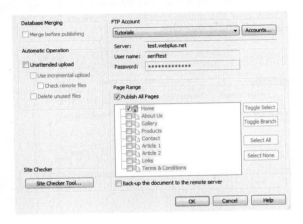 **Publish to Web**.

4. The **Publish to Web** dialog displays your FTP account details.

   If you haven't yet created an account, see Setting up your FTP on p. 111.

   In the **Page Range** tree, select which page(s) to publish. To publish the entire site, select the **Publish All Pages** option. Click **OK**.

WebPlus will convert your design into HTML pages with associated graphics and other files, then begin to upload your site to the Internet, showing individual file progress and overall progress.

Subsequent uploads of your site to that account will allow you to perform either an **Incremental Update** or a **Full Upload**.

- **Incremental Update:** If you choose this option, WebPlus will export your site and compare the exported files to those already on the server. It will only upload files that are new or have changed since the last upload. This option can also check for missing files. Incremental updates are great when you want to quickly replace minor elements of your site!

- **Full Upload:** If you choose this option, WebPlus will upload all the files, regardless of whether they have changed since the last upload.

  In both cases you can instruct WebPlus to delete uploaded files that are no longer required by selecting this option in the dialog.

5. WebPlus exports the selected pages.

   Close the **Uploading files** dialog—the **Website Publishing** dialog opens. To view your site online, choose your browser from the drop-down list and click **View this URL**.

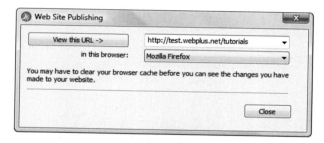

Setting up your FTP:

1. To set up a manual FTP account for the first time, using account details given by your own Internet Service Provider, in the **Publish to Web** dialog, click **Accounts...**.

2. Click **Add...** to open the **Account Details** dialog.

   When publishing to the Web (or uploading it manually using FTP software) you'll need to provide the following information, most of which you can obtain from your Internet Service Provider (ISP) or Web host:

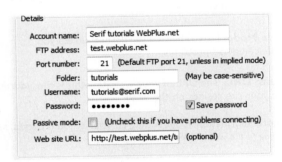

- **Account name:** A descriptive name for this connection. This can be any name of your choice. You'll use it to identify this account in WebPlus (you may have more than one).

- **FTP address:** The URL (path), similar to a Web address, that locates the Internet-based server that will store your files.

  This will start with 'ftp://' and is supplied by your service provider.

- **Port number:** Unless directed by your provider, leave the **Port number** set at 21. This is the default port used by most FTP servers for file transfer.

- **Folder:** Allows you to upload sites to sub-folders of your main website's address. You can leave this blank unless you are directed otherwise by your provider, or you want to publish to a specific subfolder of your root directory. (This may also be needed to correctly route your upload specifically to your own Web space.)

- **Username:** Specified by your ISP or Web host (and is often case-sensitive).

- **Password:** As for Username, this is normally the same information required for ISP or Web host account log-on, and is often case-sensitive.

- **Passive Mode:** Leave checked (by default) unless you experience upload problems.

- **Website URL:** The URL of your website—this is the 'address' where your site resides on the Web.

  For more information about setting up your account details, see *Publishing to the web* in WebPlus Help

3. When you've entered all your information, click **OK**.

4. Click **Update Account**, your new FTP account and settings are displayed in the **Publish to Web** dialog.

5. In the **Page Range** tree, select which page(s) to publish. To publish the entire site, select the **Publish All Pages** option. Click **OK**.

For more information, see WebPlus Help.

To convert file names:

If your web server cannot accommodate spaces in file names, complete the following steps to have WebPlus remove the spaces and symbols from file names when they are published:

1. On the **File** menu, click **Site Properties**.

2. Click the **File Naming** category and then select the **Remove spaces** and **Remove symbol character** options.

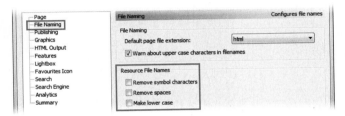

3. Web pages are normally published with lower case file names. Select **Make lower case** to get WebPlus to do this for you.

4. If you've already published your site, you'll need to republish to fix the problem. This also improves site reliability.

That's it! You've published your site to the Web for all to see! As you can see, WebPlus makes it very easy to publish your site and upload new content.

⚠ If you're having problems we suggest you check your provider's website to find the information you need, or contact their customer support team.

Note: Serif cannot supply you with this information unless you have a Serif web hosting account.

Photo Galleries

With WebPlus, you can add stunning photo galleries to your websites. Simply add your photos, and then choose from a range of professionally-designed templates. You can customize the templates to suit the theme of your photos, and even add background music!

By the end of this tutorial you will be able to:

- Create a photo gallery.

- Add photos to a photo gallery.

- Organize photos within a photo gallery.

- Add captions to photos.

- Apply gallery styles and settings.

- Edit an existing photo gallery.

- Add hyperlinks to photos.

Let's begin...

- On the **File** menu, click **New**.

  - or -

  In the Startup Wizard, in the Create section, click **Start New Site**.

A new blank document opens with a single page displayed in the **Site** tab.

Types of photo gallery

WebPlus offers three types of photo gallery, each with their own unique set of features—here's a brief overview to help you decide which gallery best suits your needs.

Professional Flash™, **Flash™** and **JavaScript** photo galleries each offer different gallery styles and settings for you to determine user navigation.

Professional Flash is more suitable for displaying large photo collections—you can present your photos in multiple albums. It offers horizontal thumbnail rollover styles which enable you to define basic preferences, as well as settings for captions, navigation bars, albums and hyperlinks. By enabling advanced options you can also define your preferences for gallery transitions, timers, and text. You can load images into the gallery from an RSS 2.0 Media feed or SlideShowPro Director content system, and export your preferred gallery settings to file so that you can import them to use whenever you create a Professional Flash gallery.

Flash is ideal for displaying smaller photo collections and **JavaScript** is a suitable alternative to using Flash™ on your site. They both offer horizontal and vertical thumbnail rollover, photo grid and photo stack styles. You can define settings for gallery position, thumbnails, navigation bars, captions and transitions. With Flash only, you can also add background music.

Creating a photo gallery

For this exercise, you'll need a selection of your own photographs or images, perhaps choosing ones which fit well with your website theme. We'll create a photo gallery using photographs taken on a visit to a falconry centre and place this on a new blank website, but you may want to add yours to an existing WebPlus project.

To create a photo gallery:

1. On the Standard Objects toolbar, on the ▼ Picture flyout, click **Insert Photo Gallery**.

2. In the **Photo Gallery** dialog, select the type of gallery you want to use:

    - Professional Flash Photo Gallery

    - Flash Photo Gallery

    - JavaScript Gallery

      The procedure for adding a photo gallery to your site is the same for all three types of gallery. For this exercise, we've selected a **Professional Flash Photo Gallery**.

3. Click **Next**.

Adding and organizing your photos

The second window in the Photo Gallery dialog allows you to add and organize your gallery photos.

To add photos to a photo gallery:

1. In the **Photo Gallery** dialog, click 📁 **Add Folder**.

2. In the **Browse For Folder** dialog, select the folder containing your photos and click **OK**.

    Your photos display as thumbnails in the dialog.

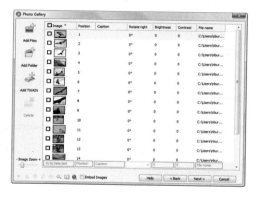

3. The buttons running down the left side of the dialog offer the following options:

    *   **Add Files**: Choose this option to add individual photos to your gallery.

    *   **Add Folder**: Choose this option to add photos contained inside a folder on your computer.

- **Add TWAIN**: Choose this option to add photos from a TWAIN source, such as a scanner or digital camera. (For details, see WebPlus Help.)

- **Delete**: Choose this option to delete selected photos that you no longer want.

With all the photographs now added, we can organize and edit them to help the gallery content flow better.

To organize photos within the gallery:

1. Use the buttons across the lower edge of the dialog to adjust image order, rotate images, edit albums, edit hyperlinks, and embed images.

We want our photo gallery to begin with the photo of the European Long-Eared Eagle Owl. Currently this photo is at number 13 in the sequence so we need to move it.

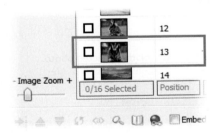

2. Select the photo check box and then click ⇥ **Move to Position**.

In the **Move To** dialog, input the number **1** and then click **OK**, to move the photo to first place in the sequence.

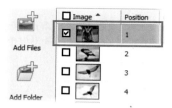

If you need to, zoom into your images using the **Image Zoom** slider.

3. (Optional) To embed your photos in the .wpp project file, select the **Embed Images** check box. (If you do not select this option your photos will remain 'linked' to the file.)

Now let's add some captions to our photos.

To add a caption to a photo:

1. With the first photo still selected, click the **Caption** column.

2. In the **Caption** box type a caption for the selected photo.

3. Repeat steps 1 and 2 to add captions to the remaining photos.

   - or -

   To add the same caption to multiple photos, select their check boxes and type the caption into the box at the bottom of the **Caption** column.

When you are happy with the photos in the gallery, their order and their captions, click **Next**.

Applying gallery styles and settings

Each gallery type offers a variety of professionally-designed preset template styles for you to choose from and modify to suit your needs.

To apply gallery styles and settings:

1. Click through the templates displayed in the **Gallery Style** pane.

As you do so:

-   The Preview pane shows how your photos will appear with the selected gallery style applied.

- The settings pane updates to display the various options you can adjust for the selected gallery style.

2. Select the gallery style you prefer and then adjust the settings as required. When you are happy with your photo gallery style and settings, click **Finish**.

3. Click once on your page to insert the gallery at default size.

 Don't forget to save your work!

Previewing your photo gallery

Now your photo gallery is created and added to your page, let's see what it looks like!

To preview your photo gallery:

1. On the Standard toolbar, click the arrow to expand the 🖵 ▾ **Preview Site** drop-down list.

2. Select **Preview Site in {your web browser of choice}**.

Editing your photo gallery and adjusting photos

Once you've inserted your photo gallery, it's easy to resize and move it on the site.

To resize and move a photo gallery:

- To resize the photo gallery, select it with the ↖ **Pointer Tool** and drag from a corner or line end handle. To constrain the photo gallery when resizing, hold down the **Shift** key when dragging.

Javascript galleries cannot be resized using the above method. The size of the Javascript gallery must be set in the final window of the **Photo Gallery** dialog.

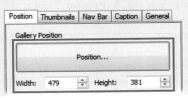

- To move the position of the photo gallery on your page, select it with the ⚲ **Pointer Tool** and drag.

Once you've placed the gallery on the page and previewed it, you may wish to make some changes. You can easily add, delete and organize gallery photos, switch to a different gallery style, and adjust gallery settings whenever you need.

To edit a photo gallery:

1. Right click the photo gallery and click **Edit Photo Gallery...**.

    - or -

    Double-click the photo gallery using the ⚲ **Pointer Tool**.

2. The **Photo Gallery** dialog opens.

3. To fine-tune your gallery, follow the steps outlined in previous sections.

Adding hyperlinks

Although a photo gallery can simply be used to display your photos, it can also act as a navigation tool to point visitors towards more information about the contents of the photo. This is achieved by adding a hyperlink.

In our example, each photo links to a new website page with more information about the bird of prey pictured.

To add hyperlinks to photos:

1. Click **Edit Hyperlink.**

2. In the **Edit Hyperlinks** dialog, select **Use a different link...** from the **Hyperlink Type** drop-down list.

3. Click **OK**.

4. Select the photo check box and then double-click the **Hyperlink** column.

    - or -

    To add the same hyperlink to multiple photos, select their check boxes and then double-click the hyperlink box at the bottom of the **Hyperlink** column.

5. In the **Hyperlinks** dialog, select **Site Page** option, then select a site page from the **Page name** drop-down list.

6. Click **OK**.

We've reached the end of this tutorial. With some simple steps, we've created a stylish, professional-looking photo gallery. We're sure you'll enjoy experimenting with this powerful feature—a great way to display treasured memories, showcase artistic shots, or sell your products!

 For more information on using your website and images to sell products, see the tutorial *E-Commerce* on p. 173.

Flash Objects

Flash™ (*.swf) files are viewable movies which use the Flash Player format for playback. Using WebPlus, it's very easy to add your own custom Flash objects to your WebPlus site.

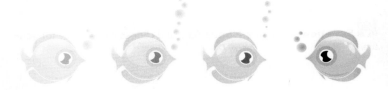

By the end of this tutorial you will be able to:

- Insert a custom Flash object into a WebPlus site.

- Fine-tune your Flash object.

Go to **http://go.serif.com/resources/WPX5** to download the following tutorial project file(s):
- **scuba.wpp**
- **fish.swf**

Let's begin...

1.   On the Standard toolbar, click 📂 **Open**.

2.   Navigate to the **scuba.wpp** file, select it and click **Open**.

     The 'Home' page is displayed in the workspace.

💾 **Save now!** Click **File > Save As...** and choose a new name for your file.

Adding a Flash object

Adding a custom Flash object to your WebPlus site is very straightforward and you can see the effects of these files as soon as they are placed on your page, even without previewing.

So let's see how easy it really is. We'll add an animation of a fish to the bottom, right-hand corner of the Scuba Home page.

We've added additional content to the **scuba.wpp** example above. For information on adding content, see the tutorial *Pictures* on p. 59.

To insert a custom Flash file:

1. On the **Insert** menu, choose **Media**, and then click **Flash**.

    - or -

    On the Web Objects toolbar, on the 🎵 ▾ Media flyout, click 🄵 **Flash...**

2. In the **Flash** dialog, click **Browse**, and then locate and select **fish.swf**.

3. (Optional) To keep the .swf file separate from the WebPlus file (using a link to the source file) clear the **Embed Flash file in site** option.

4. Click **OK**.

5. On the WebPlus page, you'll see the ⬛ **Picture Import** cursor.

    Click to insert the file at its default size, or drag to set a custom size. You should see a preview of the file as you drag.

Remember, you can always resize a Flash object once you have placed it on your page.

Congratulations! You have successfully added the Flash object to your website. Why not preview it in your favourite browser?

 Don't forget to save your work!

Previewing your Flash object

Now your Flash object is added to your site, let's see what it looks like!

To preview your Flash object:

1. On the Standard toolbar, click the arrow to expand the 🖥 ▾
    Preview Site drop-down list.

2. Select **Preview Site in {your web browser of choice}**.

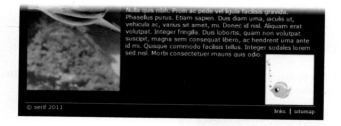

Fine-tuning your Flash object

This particular Flash file has a white background which looks unsightly against the colour scheme of the Scuba site. Also, the animation only plays once, meaning the fish soon stops swimming.

These problems can be quickly rectified by editing the Flash object's display properties.

To edit a Flash object:

1. Right click the Flash object and click **Edit Flash....**

    - or -

    Double-click the photo gallery using the ➤ **Pointer Tool**.

2. In the **Flash** dialog, in the **Display** section:

    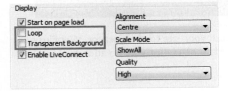

    *   To make the animation play continuously, select the **Loop** check box.

    *   To remove white backgrounds from the Flash object, select the **Transparent Background** check box.

        This will make all white background areas transparent while displayed on your site. The original file is unaffected.

3. (Optional) Set the **Alignment**, **Scale Mode**, and export **Quality** of the Flash object using the respective drop-down lists.

4. When you have finished fine-tuning the settings, click **OK**.

The valid parameters for Flash objects vary depending on the object itself. For details, see the documentation relating to your particular Flash object.

When previewed, the Flash object now blends in perfectly with the Scuba background and the fish swims inexhaustibly back and forth.

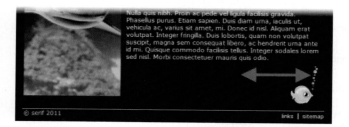

Should you choose to publish your site to the Internet, WebPlus will automatically upload your Flash object for you; no additional work is required on your behalf.

Panels I: Designing with Panels

Panels have special properties which allow background elements to be stretched to fit the panel size. This makes designing a consistent look and feel for your site a really easy job! In this tutorial, we'll look at the use of panels as design elements.

By the end of this tutorial you will be able to:

- Create a panel.

- Create a panel background.

- Create a stretching design.

- Create a fixed design.

- Insert a previously created design.

Let's begin...

- On the **File** menu, click **New**.

  - or -

  In the Startup Wizard, in the Create section, click **Start New Site**.

A new blank document opens with a single page displayed in the **Site** tab.

 In order to look at the different ways of using panels, we are not going to work to any particular design scheme. Instead, we'll work through a series of examples that should give you the tools you need in order to apply panels to your own site.

Creating panels as design elements

When designing a website, you always want to aim for a consistent look and feel. This can be seen in the example below.

If you are quite adventurous with your design, you may find that it's a slow process trying to get everything to look the same. This is where the special properties of panels can help.

In this first example, we'll create a panel similar to the Popular Tags panel illustrated above. All design editing for panels is done in the dedicated environment of the **Design Studio**.

To begin a new panel design:

1. On the Web Object toolbar, in the Navigation flyout, click ☐ **Insert Panel**.

2. In the dialog, next to the background drop-down menu, click 🖉 .

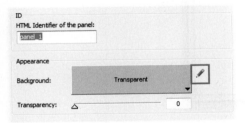

The Design Studio opens to a blank (transparent) panel.

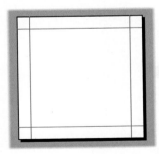

The next step is to start the design.

To create a panel background:

1. On the Standard Objects toolbar, on the ⬚▾ QuickShapes flyout, click the ⬚ **Quick Rectangle**.

2. Starting in the top left corner, drag on the page to draw a shape that covers most of the transparent panel. Ensure that the edges of the QuickShape are placed in between the grid lines.

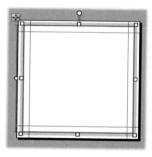

3. On the **Swatches** tab, click the ⬚ **Fill** and then click the **Scheme 2** swatch.

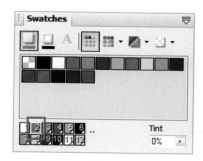

The fill updates.

4. Drag the node control downwards to round the corners of the QuickShape.

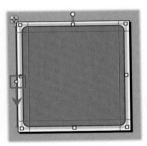

5. Before we finish, let's change the colour scheme. On the **Swatches** tab, click " to open the **Scheme Designer**.

6. Select the **Melancholy** scheme, click **Load** and then **OK** to exit. Our schemed object is updated to the new colours.

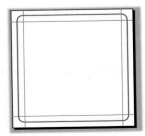

7. On the Standard toolbar, click ✓ **Commit Changes** to exit the **Design Studio**.

8. In the **Panel Properties** dialog, click **OK** to accept the default settings and exit.

9. Place the ⊹▣ cursor and click once to insert the panel at the default size.

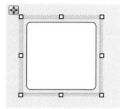

- or -

Click and drag on the page to set the panel size manually.

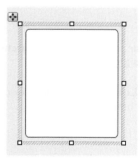

⚠ **Save now!** Click **File > Save As...** and choose a new name for your file.

Special design properties

Take a moment to resize the panel by dragging on one of the resize handles. Notice that the corners always remain the same shape. This is because they were placed within the grid lines when we drew the object. We can use the special properties of the gridlines to create more advanced designs.

Let's do this now.

To create a stretching panel design:

1. Click the panel, then on the Panel context toolbar, click **Edit Panel** (or select **Edit Panel...** from the right-click menu).

2. In the dialog, next to the background drop-down menu, click to open the **Design Studio**.

3. On the Standard Objects toolbar, on the QuickShapes flyout, click the **Quick Rectangle**.

4. Drag on the page to create a long, thin rectangle inside the existing background shape. This will make the surrounding box for our heading text. Drag the node control up to create the cut out corner effect.

Don't worry that the shape doesn't fit within the guides at this time as we can change this when we've completed the design.

5. With the shape selected, on the **Align** tab, ensure that **Relative to: Page** is selected and then click ♎ **Centre Horizontally**.

6. On the **Line** tab, in the drop-down list, change the line type to a double line.

7. On the **Swatches** tab, click ▦ **Fill** and then click the **Scheme 7** swatch. Next, click ▬ **Line** and then click the **Scheme 8** swatch. The shape is updated.

Now we need to change the guides so that the shape is enclosed.

8. Drag the horizontal guide down so that the entire shape is contained within the new guide area.

This will prevent the shape from changing height when we resize the panel. However, we also want the two ends of the shape to stay the same if we change the width of the panel.

9. Drag each vertical guide inwards so that the left and right edges of the shape are contained within the vertical guides as illustrated.

This will 'fix' the corners in place, but sill allow the centre of the design to stretch or contract as necessary.

10. On the Standard toolbar, click ✓ **Commit Changes** to exit the Design Studio.

11. In the **Panel Properties** dialog, click **OK** to accept the default settings and exit.

On the page, you'll see that the panel design has been updated to reflect our changes. If you resize the panel, you'll see that the header design changes to fit the width of the panel, but never changes in depth.

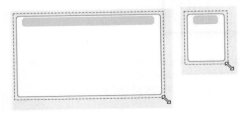

Don't forget to save your work!

Finally, we'll place a small design in the bottom corner of our panel.

To place a fixed design object on a panel:

1. Click the panel, then on the Panel context toolbar, click 🔲 **Edit Panel** (or select **Edit Panel...** from the right-click menu).

2. In the dialog, next to the background drop-down menu, click 🖊 to open the **Design Studio**.

3. On the Standard Objects toolbar, on the 🔲▾ QuickShapes flyout, click the ✿ **Quick Petal**.

4. Drag on the page to create a shape approximately 35 pix by 35 pix and position it as illustrated.

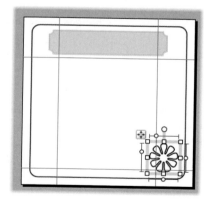

Notice that the shape does not quite fit within the grid lines. If we leave it like this and accepted our design, we'd start to get some strange behaviour if we changed the shape of our panel.

So what can we do to change this? We can't update the guides in the same way as before as this would affect our heading design. Instead, we need to fix the shape.

5. In the **Design Studio**, ensure that the QuickShape is selected.

6. On the Design Studio toolbar, in the ⊞ ▾ Horizontal scale flyout, click ⊞ **Right**.

7. On the Design Studio toolbar, in the ⊟ ▾ Vertical scale flyout, click ⊟ **Bottom**.

8. On the Standard toolbar, click ✓ **Commit Changes** to exit the Design Studio.

9. In the **Panel Properties** dialog, click **OK** to accept the default settings and exit.

On the page, you'll see that the panel design has been updated to reflect our changes. If you resize the panel, you'll see that the header design changes to fit the width of the panel, but the QuickShape always stays the same size and in the same place.

To insert a previously created design:

1. On the Web Object toolbar, in the 🔡 ▾ Navigation flyout, click ☐ **Insert Panel**.

2. In the dialog, click the arrow to view the **Background** flyout.

3. In the **Site** category, select the design that we created earlier.

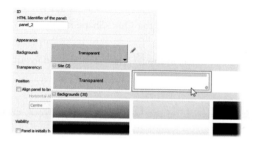

4. Click **OK** to accept the default settings.

5. Place the ⊕▦ cursor and click once to insert the panel at the default size.

    - or -

    Click and drag on the page to set the panel size manually.

Once you have created your panels, you add your content! Why not have a look at the next tutorial *Panels II: Assigning actions* on p. 147.

Panels II: Assigning Actions

In the previous tutorial, we looked at panels as design elements. Panels have special properties which mean that they can have actions assigned to them. They can be made to hide until an item is clicked or hovered over, they can be free-floating, they can even be set to remain in view even when the window is scrolled! It makes the panel a really useful tool. In this tutorial we'll look at a few of the useful functions.

By the end of this tutorial you will be able to:

- Attach a floating panel to a browser window.

- Add objects to a panel.

- Add visibility actions.

- Hide and position a panel.

Let's begin...

- On the **File** menu, click **New**.

  - or -

  In the Startup Wizard, in the Create section, click **Start New Site**.

A new blank document opens with a single page displayed in the **Site** tab.

 In order to look at the different ways of using panels, we are not going to work to any particular design scheme. Instead, we'll work through a series of examples that should give you the tools you need in order to apply panels to your own site.

Floating panels

One use for a panel is as a 'floating' object that is permanently attached to the browser window and on view. These can be attached to the browser window, meaning that they do not scroll with the page. The main reason for this is to have a navigation bar that is always accessible, either at the side of the top of the window.

To add a panel to a page:

1. On the Web Object toolbar, in the ⊞▾ Navigation flyout, click ☐ **Insert Panel**.

2. In the dialog, click the arrow to view the **Background** flyout.

3. In the **Backgrounds** category, select the first design and click **OK** to accept the default settings and exit.

4. Starting at the top left of the page, click and drag on the page to create a panel approximately 90 pix high and spans the width of the page.

To make it easy to see what's going on when we make changes to our panel, we'll add a placeholder frame to our page.

To add a placeholder frame:

1. On the Standard Objects toolbar, in the ⊞▾ Text Frames flyout, click the ⊞ **HTML Text Frame Tool**.

2. Click and drag on the page to insert the frame that fills the blank space on the page.

3. On the **Insert** menu, click **Fill with Placeholder Text**.

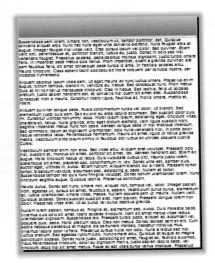

Previewing the (scrolling) panel:

1. On the Standard toolbar, click the arrow to expand the 🖥️ ▾ **Preview Site** drop-down list.

2. Click the **Preview in Window (Internet Explorer)** option.

3. Drag the scroll bar up and down. Notice that the panel also scrolls out of view. We can change this in the panel properties.

4. Click ⊠ **Close Preview** to return to the open document.

To attach panel to a browser window:

1. Click the panel, then on the Panel context toolbar, click ⬛ **Edit Panel** (or select **Edit Panel...** from the right-click menu).

2. In the **Panel Properties** dialog, select the **Align panel to browser window**.

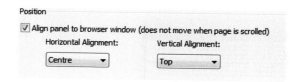

3. The default alignment options are **Centre** and **Top**. These are ideal for our needs so click **OK** to accept the changes.

Preview the page again and drag the scroll bar up and down. Notice that the panel no longer scrolls. However, the text scrolls over the top of the panel which isn't ideal. To stop this, we need to change the z-order of the panel.

Click ⊠ **Close Preview** to return to the open document.

To bring the panel to the top of the z-order:

*   Select the panel and on the **Arrange** toolbar, click **Bring to Front**.

Preview the page again and drag the scroll bar up and down. The text now scrolls neatly behind the panel.

To complete the panel, all you need to do is add a navigation bar! A panel behaves like a container, so when an object is added on top of a panel, it inherits the panel properties. Try it out for yourself!

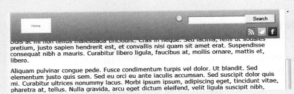

Panels and master pages

It's common practice to place navigation elements on a master page so that it's easy to achieve consistency throughout your website. However, if you do this and still want your navigation panel to be permanently on view on top of your content, then you need to remember to adjust the order of the master page in the **Objects** tab. To do this, display the **Objects** tab and then drag the master page containing your panel and navigation bar (Master A in this example) to the top of the stack.

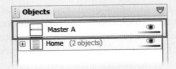

All objects placed on the master page will now display on top of your content. You will need to do this for each page that uses the master page. For more information on using master pages, see WebPlus Help.

Hidden panels

Panels can also be hidden until some action is performed, normally either a click or a hover-over. This means that they can be used to display extra information while keeping your visitor on a specific page. They can also be used for surveys and advertisements. It's also possible to have a panel on view when a visitor enters your site and then provide a button for them to close (hide) the panel.

When creating hidden panels, it's always best to design your panel before you hide it!

To create a basic panel:

1. On the Web Object toolbar, in the Navigation flyout, click ☐ **Insert Panel**.

2. In the **Backgrounds** category, select a basic design (we chose plain white) and click **OK** to accept the default settings and exit.

3. Place the ⁺◼ cursor and click once to insert the panel at the default size.

    - or -

    Click and drag on the page to set the panel size manually.

To make our panel useful, we'll need to add some elements. Panels can contain virtually anything—images, text, QuickShapes, buttons, galleries, smart objects, advertisements... You'll need to think carefully about what you're trying to do by using a panel. For now we'll just add an image and a gallery object.

To add objects to a panel:

1. On the Standard Objects toolbar, on the ⬛▾ Picture flyout, click ⊠ **Empty Picture Frame** and place your empty frame inside the panel. Add an image to the frame. (See the tutorial *Pictures* on p. 59 for detailed information.)

2. Next, on the **Gallery** tab, expand the **Icon Sets** > **Bright** category and drag the red cross to the top right corner of the panel.

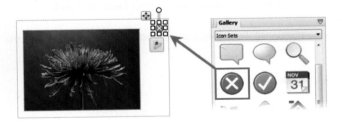

Our panel is now complete. If you preview it in a browser, you'll see that it doesn't really do anything exciting. Let's apply an action to the close button that we added.

To add an action to an object:

1. Right-click on the cross object that we added to the panel and in the menu, click **Actions...**

2. In the **Actions** dialog, click **Add...** and from the drop-down list, click **Visibility**.

3. In the **Show/Hide Panel Action** dialog:

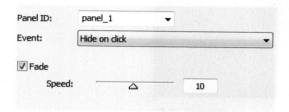

- Select the panel to apply the action to from the **Panel ID** drop-down list. (We only have a single panel in this example.)

- In the **Event** drop-down list, select **Hide on Click**.

- (Optional) To increase or decrease the fade speed, adjust the slider.

- Click **OK**.

4. The assigned actions are displayed in the **Actions** dialog.

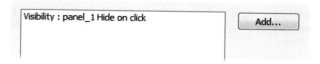

5. Click **OK** to return to the page.

6. Preview your panel in a browser. If you click on the cross, the panel should disappear. This is useful behaviour for advertising panels but you'll notice that we now have no way of reopening our panel. (If you still have your preview open, close it now.)

7. On the **Gallery** tab, expand the **Icon Sets** > **Standard** category and drag the polaroid photo icon to the **page**. (Ensure that it doesn't touch or overlap the panel.) Resize it so it's about double its original size.

We're now going to add a visibility action to the new object.

8. Right-click on the new object and in the menu, click **Actions...**

9. In the **Actions** dialog, click **Add...** and from the drop-down list, click **Visibility**.

10. In the **Show/Hide Panel Action** dialog:

    •   Select the panel to apply the action to from the **Panel ID** drop-down list. (We only have a single panel in this example.)

    •   In the **Event** drop-down list, select **Show on Click**.

    •   (Optional) To increase or decrease the fade speed, adjust the slider.

    •   Click **OK**.

11. The assigned actions are displayed in the **Actions** dialog.

If you preview your panel again, you'll see that clicking on the cross closes the panel, and clicking on the photo icon opens it again. Well done, you've created a panel with actions!

Now that we've created our panel and tested our design, we can hide the panel when the page first opens. If you still have your preview open, close it now.

To hide and position a panel:

1. Click the panel, then on the Panel context toolbar, click 🔲 **Edit Panel** to open the **Panel Properties** dialog.

2. Select the **Panel is initially hidden** option and click **OK**.

    The page updates to show a hidden panel object (green question mark icon) instead of the panel.

3. Drag the hidden panel object into position next to the photo icon. This sets the position of the top-left corner of the panel when it opens.

4. Finally, with the hidden panel object still selected, on the **Arrange** toolbar, click **Bring to Front**.

This ensures that the panel opens on top of the photo icon.

5. Preview the panel to test out it's new functionality!

 You can also quick hide or show the panel by selecting the panel and then clicking ⬚ **Hide Panel** on the Panel context toolbar.

That's all there is to it. You should now have everything you need to create various panels in your own website. Good luck and have fun! For information on designing with panels, don't forget to have a look at the *Panels I: Using Panels in Design* tutorial on p. 135.

Contact Forms

Web-based forms are useful tools. In this tutorial, we're going to add a contact form to a 'Contact Us' page that we created on our fictional SCUBA diving club site to allow site visitors to contact the webmaster and submit their personal comments.

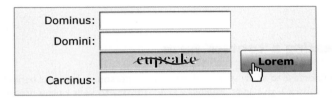

By the end of this tutorial you will be able to:

- Create a web-based email contact form.

- Edit form objects.

- Display a form page in a lightbox object.

⚠ This tutorial assumes that you have already registered for a **Serif Web Resources** account as you will need to log in to access the Smart objects. If you are unsure how to do this, see the tutorial *Serif Web Resources* or see WebPlus Help.

🔽 Go to **http://go.serif.com/resources/WPX5** to download the following tutorial project file(s):
  🔵 **scuba.wpp**

Let's begin...

1. On the Standard toolbar, click 📂 **Open**.

2. Navigate to the **scuba.wpp** file, select it and click **Open**.

    The 'Home' page is displayed in the workspace.

Creating a 'contact' form

It's important to show visitors there is a live person or business behind your website—this adds credibility and legitmacy to your online presence.

By providing easy ways for visitors to communicate with you, you will establish this credibility. You may wish to add your postal address, telephone numbers and email address to your website, though this carries with it the risk of unwanted spam.

Instead we recommend providing visitors with a secure contact form for them to contact you directly.

 Forms can be used to collect a variety of data from site visitors. Data collected can be as simple as the person's name and email address, or a whole host of personal information. How much data you ask for on a form really depends on what you need it for.

Let's get started.

To create a contact form using the Form Wizard:

1. Open the **Contact** page in the workspace by double-clicking it on the **Site** tab.

> You'll notice that this page is different to the others in the site. It is smaller and does not use a Master Page. This is because we want to display it in a Lightbox—a self-contained window that floats above your web page. See WebPlus Help for more details.

2. On the Web Objects toolbar, on the ⊟▾ Forms flyout, click ⊟ **Form Wizard**.

3. In the first **Form Wizard** dialog, click **Use and adapt a standard form** and then click **Next**.

4. Click any list item to display a preview of the selected form in the **Preview** pane.

Select the **Comments 2** form and click **Next**.

5. The next dialog screen allows you to customize the form layout and add additional items. The default layout is almost right, but we need to add a captcha object. Click the **CAPTCHA** button.

6. In the **Add New Control** dialog, type "Are you human? Type the letters you see." in the **Enter label** box and click **OK**.

The new object is displayed at the bottom of the list.

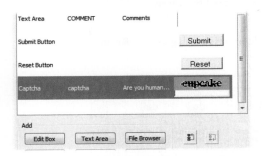

7. Next, with the captcha object select, click 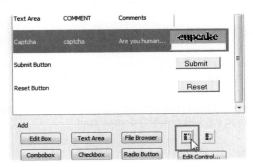 **Move Up** twice to move the object above the Submit Button.

8.   Click **Next**.

Form controls

The building blocks of a form comprise a mixture of text, graphics, and **form controls**. Form controls collect visitor data and can be added, moved, and modified in a similar way to other WebPlus objects.

Form control fields include buttons, text boxes, check boxes, radio buttons, combo boxes, and so on. A typical form is made up of a combination of these fields.

The captcha object is linked to your Serif Web Resources account and is an anti-spamming control. It helps to prevent junk email from non-human web traffic. The site visitor must type the graphical word into the input field. If they match, the visitor is allowed to continue.

9.   In the **Form Properties** dialog, on the **Action** dialog:

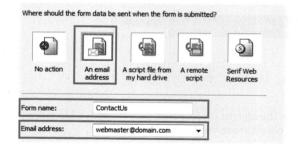

   •   Select **An e-mail address**.

   •   Type a name for your form. (This must not contain spaces or special characters.)

   •   Type the email address to which you want the site visitor's form data to be sent, e.g. webmaster@domain.com

   •   Click **Finish**.

10. To insert the form at default size, position the ⊹ cursor where you want the form to appear and then click once.

Don't forget to save your work!

11. On the Standard toolbar, click the arrow to expand the 🖳▾ **Preview Site** drop-down list.

12. Select **Preview Page in {your web browser of choice}** to see what your form will look like.

Editing form layout

You'll notice that some of the objects don't look that good:

- The form field labels are too dark and don't stand out.

- The captcha object label is too long.

- The form **Submit** and **Reset** buttons don't line up with the other input fields.

- There is no title!

Luckily, WebPlus lets you move and edit form controls just as you would any other object. We'll demonstrate this now...

To move and edit form buttons and labels:

1. Select the captcha object label and drag the corner handle to resize it.

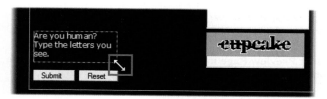

2. Drag a selection marquee over the input fields to select them all and then drag them into place next to the text.

3. Next, drag a selection marquee around all of the text labels.

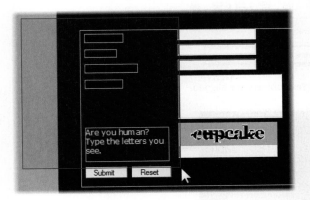

Form labels are simply HTML text frames. This means that you can edit them in exactly the same way as an HTML frame that you place on the page.

4. On the **Swatches** tab, click the Scheme 11 swatch.

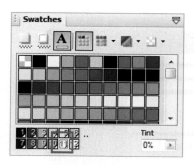

5. On the **Align** tab ensure that **Relative to: Selection** is displayed, and click the **Right** align button.

The text objects are aligned.

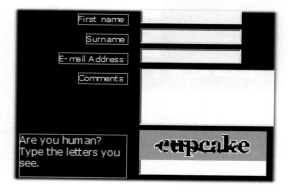

6. Finally, select both the **Submit** and the **Reset** button and drag them into place below the captcha object.

🖎 We also added an HTML text frame to the top of our form to create a title. The text was set to Heading 2.

⚠️ **Don't forget to save your work!**

7. On the Standard toolbar, click the arrow to expand the 🖥️▾ **Preview Site** drop-down list.

8. Select **Preview Page in {your web browser of choice}** to see what your form will look like.

Displaying a form in a lightbox

- Double-click on the 'Home' page on the **Site** tab.

If you look carefully at the **Site** tab, you'll notice that the Contact page is not included in the navigation. Instead, we're going to link to it from the 'contact us' text at the top of the Master page.

To link a form page to a lightbox:

1. On the Home page, click the 'contact us' text object and then click **Edit on Master Page**.

2. Select all of the 'contact us' text and on the Tools toolbar, on the Hyperlink flyout, click **Insert Hyperlink**.

3. In the **Hyperlinks** dialog:

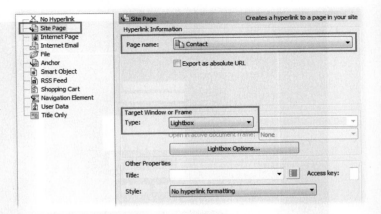

*   In the left category list click **Site Page**.

*   In the **Page Name** drop-down list select **Contact**.

*   In the **Target Window or Frame** section, select **Lightbox** from the drop-down list.

*   Click **OK**.

4. On the Standard toolbar, click the arrow to expand the 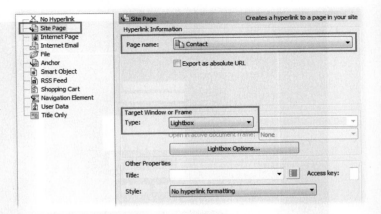 **Preview Site** drop-down list.

5. Select **Preview Site in {your web browser of choice}**.

6. Finally, click on the link to test it! Your form should display neatly in its own lightbox.

That's it! Once your form is published, visitors to your site can type their details directly into the text boxes provided. When they click **Submit**, the information is sent to the email address you specified when you created the form.

E-commerce

If you've ever bought anything online, you'll know how simple the process can be as a buyer. But how difficult is it to set up your own e-store? Fortunately with WebPlus, the process simple. Over the next few pages, we'll show you how by creating a page to sell photographic prints.

By the end of this tutorial you will be able to:

- Choose and configure your e-commerce cart provider.

- Creating an e-commerce form.

- Use an existing e-commerce form as a template for your other objects.

Go to **http://go.serif.com/resources/WPX5** to download the following tutorial project file(s):
- **scuba.wpp**

Let's begin...

1.   On the Standard toolbar, click ☞ **Open**.

2.   Navigate to the **scuba.wpp** file, select it and click **Open**.

     The 'Home' page is displayed in the workspace.

🔳 **Save now!** Click **File > Save As...** and choose a new name for your file.

In the following sections, we'll configure a shopping cart provider, and insert and configure an e-commerce form.

Choosing a Shopping Cart Provider

Any website that supports e-commerce activity will typically use a shopping cart and payment gateway. There are many third-party shopping cart providers that can be used. Each provider offers the same basic features and with WebPlus, it's easy to set up your e-commerce site using one of our selected providers, all of which offer a good range of features.

In this project, we've chosen PayPal© as the provider most suited to sell some photo prints. We'll now step you through the signup and configuration process.

Our example uses PayPal© as our shopping cart provider. Some cart providers offer additional features and depending on your needs, these may or may not be important to you. Use the provider's Help pages to find out more about unique shopping cart features.

To setup and configure a PayPal shopping cart:

1. On the Web Objects toolbar, on the 💲▾ E-commerce flyout, click
    🔳 **Configure E-commerce**.

2. In the **E-commerce Configuration** dialog, select the **PayPal**
    option and choose one of the following options:

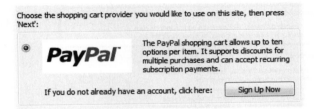

- If you already have a PayPal account, click **Next**.

- If you don't have an account, click **Sign Up Now**. The PayPal
  site opens in your browser. Follow the instructions provided to
  register and set up an account. When you have finished, return
  to WebPlus.

3. In the **PayPal Configuration** dialog:

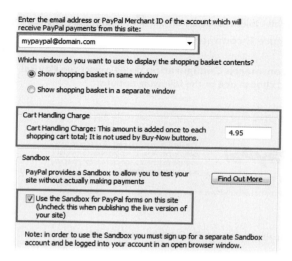

- Type the email address where you want to receive notification about payments received.

- Set the **Cart Handling Charge**, i.e. your default overall shipping charge.

- (Optional) If you want to use PayPal's **Sandbox**, a test tool for trying out your shopping cart before going live, select this option.

  To use the Sandbox, you must set up a separate test account (in addition to your live PayPal login) through PayPal's Developer Central site. Click **Find Out More** to do this.

- Click **Next**.

4. Click **Use the PayPal Minicart**.

    For now, leave the default settings (you can always change them later) and click **Finish**.

Creating an e-commerce form

WebPlus makes it really easy to add e-commerce objects, either as a form or link, depending on the characteristics of the item(s) you are selling. In our example, we'll add a form since it offers more flexibility and allows for some user interactivity.

 For information on the differences between forms and links and why you might choose one over the other, see WebPlus Help.

Our site uses **empty frames** as image placeholders. This makes it very easy to create thumbnails of our e-commerce objects and means that we can replace images very easily while retaining aspect ratio. For more information on using frames, see the tutorial *Pictures* on p.59.

To add an object image and title:

1. On the **Site** tab, double-click the **Shop** page entry to display the page.

2. On the **Media Bar**, in the rightmost drop-down list, select the **WebPlus X5 - Tutorial Images** album.

3. Drag the photo of the caves (C86110009.jpg) onto the top picture frame.

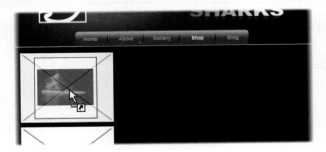

4. On the Standard Objects toolbar, in the ⊞▾ Text Frames flyout, click the ⊞ **HTML Text Frame Tool**.

5. Click and drag on the page next to the image to place an HTML frame approximately 470 pix x 30 pix, level with the top of the frame.

💡 When creating objects, the Hintline updates to show information about placement size. It also gives you other tips, tricks and shortcuts.

▤ **HTML Frame: Shift-drag** to constrain to a square. Pos: (274 pix, 380 pix) Size: (293 pix, 27 pix)

For accurate sizing, use the **Transform** tab. For more information, see WebPlus Help.

6. In the Text context toolbar, select the Heading 3 style from the drop-down list.

7. Click in the text frame and type 'The Cave print'.

We are now ready to add our e-commerce details for this print.

⚠️ **Don't forget to save your work!**

To insert a PayPal form:

1. On the Web Objects toolbar, on the 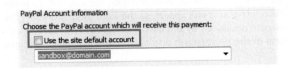 E-commerce flyout, click the **Insert an E-commerce object** button.

2. In the **Add PayPal Object** dialog:

   - Select the email address that is to receive the payment information.

   - WebPlus assumes that the email address set during shopping cart configuration is used. If you want to use a different address—for example, the address you specified when you set up your Sandbox, clear the **Use the site default address** box and select a different address to override the site default.

   PayPal Account information

   Choose the PayPal account which will receive this payment:

   ☐ Use the site default account

   sandbox@domain.com

   - Select the **Add to Shopping Cart Form** option.

   - Click **Next**.

3. In the **Button Image** dialog:

   Choose the image you would like to use for your button:

   ○ Use a standard text button   Text: Add To Cart

   ● Use a standard image

   Add to Cart   Add to Cart

   PayPal   **PayPal**
   Add To Cart   Add Item To Cart

   - Select the **Use a standard image** option.

- Select the image of your choice.

- Click **Next**.

4. In the **Item Details** dialog, enter the following information:

- **Item Name:** The name of the item for sale. Try to make this descriptive as it will appear as the item description on the invoice produced by the cart. We typed 'The Cave print'—the title of the photograph displayed in the first picture frame.

- **Item ID:** If you have a specific product code reference, enter it here. We left ours blank.

- **Currency:** Choose the currency required from the drop-down list.

- **Price:** Type the price of the item.

- Click **Next**.

5. The **Item Description** can be used to add extra details about the sale item.

- As we have three different sizes of print for sale, list the price of each size in the description.

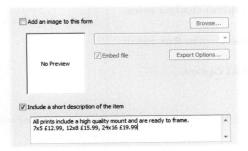

- We already have an image, so we don't need to add another. Click **Next**.

6. In the **Item Options** dialog click **Add Multiple Option...**

7. In the **Multiple Option** dialog:

- In the **Name** box, type 'Size'.

- In the **Prompt** box, type 'Size:'.

- Select **Option changes price**.

- Select the **Combo Box** option.

- Click **Add Option...**

For information on the other options in the dialog, see WebPlus Help.

8. In the **Option** dialog:

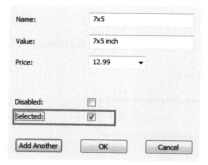

Name:	7x5
Value:	7x5 inch
Price:	12.99 ▾
Disabled:	☐
Selected:	☑

[Add Another]   [OK]   [Cancel]

- In the **Name** box, type '7x5'.

- In the **Value** box, type '7x5 inches'.

- In the **Price** drop-down list, select 12.99.

- Click the **Selected** check box—this sets the item as the default
  option when the page opens.

- Click **Add Another**.

9. Repeat step 8 to create a '12x8' option, but this time:

    • In the **Price** field, type '15.99'.

    • Do not select the **Selected** check box—you can only set one default!

    • Click **Add Another**.

10. Repeat step 9 to create a '24x16' option at '19.99' and then click **OK**.

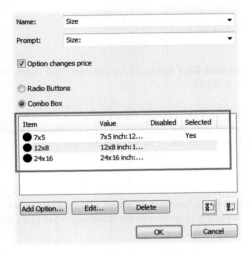

Your **Multiple Options** dialog should now list the three options you specified. Click **OK**.

11. The **Item Options** dialog displays again, allowing you to add further options. We don't want to do this so click **Next**.

12. In the **Item Details** dialog:

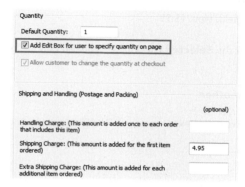

- Select the **Add Edit Box** option to let the customer define the quantity to be ordered.

- In the **Shipping and Handling** section, type the additional charges associated with the order item (if any). If these are left blank, the default profile set in PayPal will be used.

- Click **Next**.

13. In the **Extra Customer Information** dialog, ensure **Customer prompted for address** is displayed in the drop-down list and click **Next**.

14. In the **Payment Pages** dialog, leave the default settings and click **Next**.

15. In the **Form Layout** dialog, because we have more than one pricing option, clear the **Show price on form** option and click **Finish**.

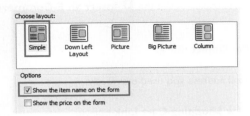

16. Click once to insert the e-commerce form on your page.

If necessary, you can move and adjust the individual form objects, and edit their appearance, as you would any other WebPlus object. We adjusted the position of the PayPal button.

Don't forget to save your work!

We're now going to insert another e-commerce object into the space created—a **View Cart** button.

To insert a View Cart button:

1. On the Web Objects toolbar, click the  **Insert an E-Commerce object** button.

2. In the **Add PayPal Object** dialog:

    •   Select the email address you used previously.

    •   Select the **View Shopping Cart Link** option.

    •   Click **Next**.

3. In the **Button Image** dialog:

    •   Select the **Use a standard image** option.

    •   Select the image you want to use.

    •   Click **Finish**.

4. Click to insert your button at default size, then drag it into position on your form.

5. Preview your page in your web browser. Check that you can:

    - Select a **Size** from the drop-down list.

    - Edit the product **Quantity**.

    - Add items to your shopping cart.

    - View your shopping cart.

Don't forget to save your work!

Using an existing form as a template

If you're happy with the way your first product looks and functions, you can use it as a template for your other objects by simply copying and editing the form.

We'll do this next...

To copy and edit the form:

1.   Drag a new picture from the **Media Bar** and onto the next empty frame.

2.   Click and drag to select the HTML print title frame and the form object.

3.   Hold the **Ctrl** key and drag down to create a copy of the objects. Position these next to the second image.

4. Click inside the new HTML title frame and change the text to 'Ocean Waves print'.

 In our sample store, we only need to change the name of each item as all other options (for example, print size and price) stay the same.

It is important that you do this by editing the form and not by editing the text boxes directly as it's the form information that gets passed to the invoice.

When you create your own e-commerce site, the extent of the changes required in these dialogs will depend on the type of items you are listing for sale. If your items are very different, you may prefer to simply create each form from scratch, rather than copying and editing your first page as we have done here.

5. Right-click on an empty part of the form and select **Edit e-commerce Form...**

6. In the **Add PayPal Object** dialog, click **Next**.

7. In the **Button Image** dialog, click **Next**.

8. In the **Items Details** dialog, check the details displayed and replace any that do not apply to your new item.

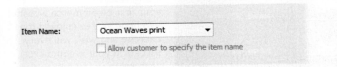

(In our case, we only needed to type in the new name for the image 'Ocean Waves'.)

Click **Next**.

9. In the **Item Description** dialog, replace any of the options that have changed for this new item. If the same options apply, as in our case, simply click **Next** to proceed.

10. Unless you need to make changes, click **Next** until you come to the **Form Layout** dialog. Ensure that the **Reformat form now** option is cleared and click **Finish**.

The form is updated with the new details.

11. Preview the page in your browser.

 Starting with empty picture frames makes it easy to create image thumbnails that have the same dimensions, without changing the aspect ratio of the pictures they contain. For more information, see the *Pictures* tutorial.

Now that you have two objects in place, it's easy to add the rest of your product list. Your finished page should look something like ours.

Congratulations, you've created your first e-commerce website! We hope you've enjoyed the exercise and wish you every success in your e-commerce ventures.

If you also worked through the other tutorials, you should by now be feeling very comfortable with WebPlus tools and well-equipped to start working on your own WebPlus creations!

2 Navigation Bars

Navigation Bars

WebPlus X5 has a selection of preset **Navigation Bars** for use in your sites. All preset navigation bars are schemed, and customizable in the all new **Button Studio**!

The following categories of presets are available:

- Block
- Graphic
- Highlight
- JavaScript
- Speech
- Standard
- Tab
- Traditional

For navigation bars of type "JavaScript", these are customizable in the **Options** and **Styles** tabs of the **Navigation Bar Settings** dialog only.

To add a preset navigation bar:

1 From the **Web Objects** toolbar's 🔲 ▾ Navigation flyout, click

 🔲 **Insert Navigation Bar.**

 - or -

 Click **Web Object>Navigation Bar...** from the **Insert** menu.

2 From the dialog's **Type** tab, browse navigation bar types in the **Type** list, expanding menu options if needed. Use the keyboard arrows for quick browsing!

 In the adjacent preview window, click on a preset to review the appearance of pop-up menus

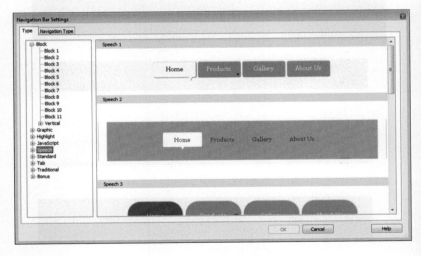

3 Select your chosen preset navigation bar and click **OK.**

The following pages provide previews of the preset **Navigation Bars** provided with **WebPlus X5**.

 For more information on adding, creating and editing **Navigation Bars** in WebPlus, please see the *Adding Navigation Bars* topic in the help, or why not try the *Navigation Bars* tutorial?

Block

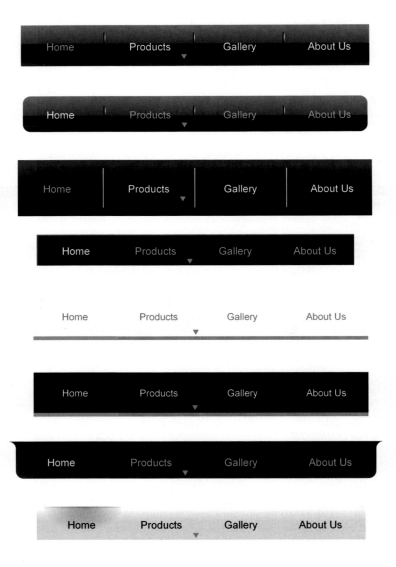

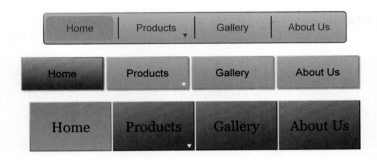

Block > Vertical

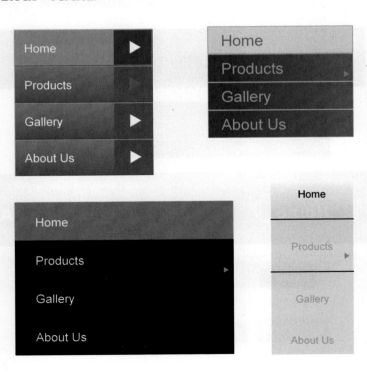

Graphic

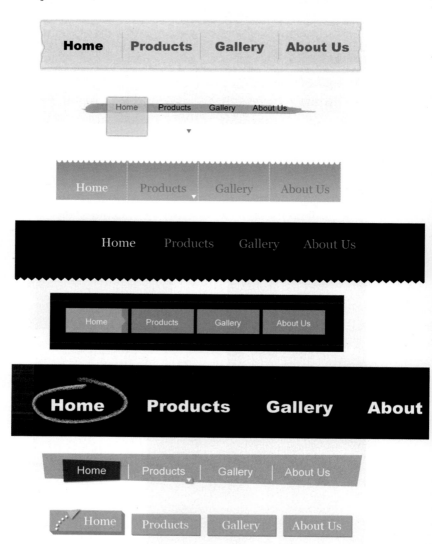

Highlight

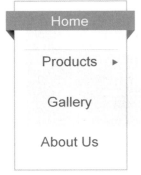

JavaScript

Home Products Gallery About Us

Home Products Gallery About Us

Home Products Gallery About Us

Home Products Gallery About Us

[Home] [Products] [Gallery] [About Us]

Home | Products | Gallery | About Us

1 | 2 | 3 | 4

Home * Products * Gallery * About Us

Home - Products - Gallery - About Us

JavaScript > Vertical

Home
Products
Gallery
About Us

Home
Products
Gallery
About Us

Home
Products
Gallery
About Us

Home
Products
Gallery
About Us

Home
Products
Gallery
About Us

JavaScript > Combo

| Home ▼ |

| Home ▼ | | Go |

JavaScript > Sitemap

Home	Home
Products	Products
New	New
Recommended	Recommended
Special Offers	Special Offers
Gallery	Gallery
About Us	About Us

JavaScript > Folding

Home	
Products	▶
Gallery	
About Us	

Speech

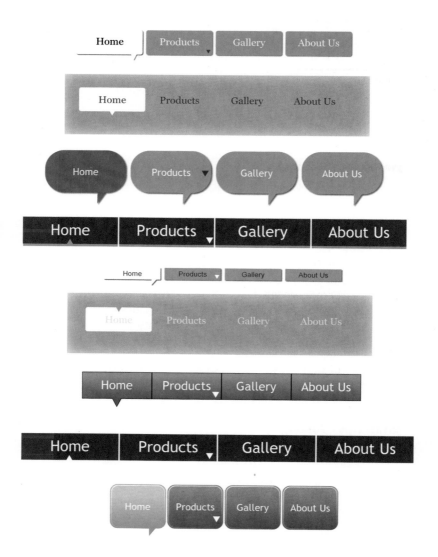

Standard

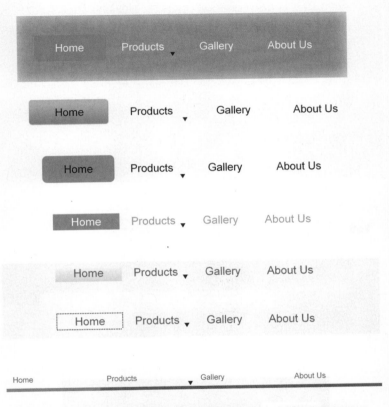

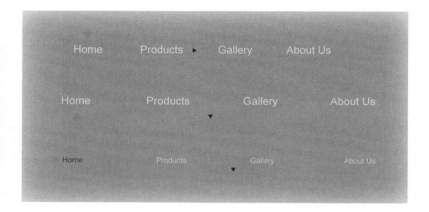

Tab

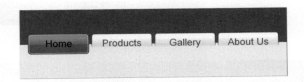

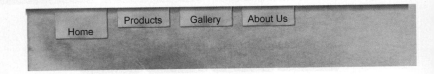

Traditional

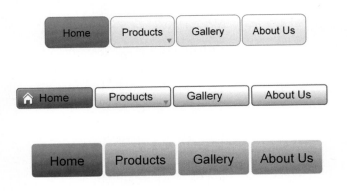

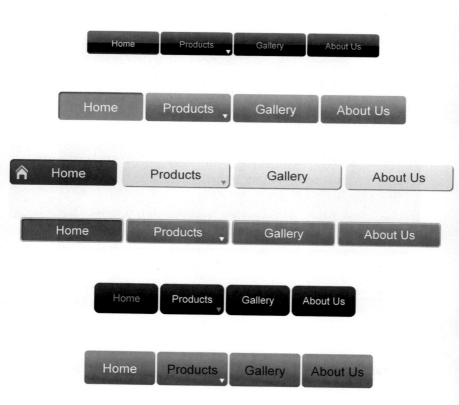

3 Colour Schemes

Using Colour Schemes

In WebPlus, a colour scheme is a group of **12** complementary colours. Schemes in WebPlus work much like a paint-by-numbers system, where page elements in a layout are assigned specific colours by number.

These colours are stored in specific swatches, numbered 1 to 12, hosted on the **Swatches** tab.

 These swatches represent the site's colour scheme. From here, you can assign colours to page elements to make them schemed.

💡 **Pro Templates**, **Theme Layouts**, preset **Navigation Bars** and some **Gallery** elements are already schemed for you!

To select a colour scheme:

1 Click 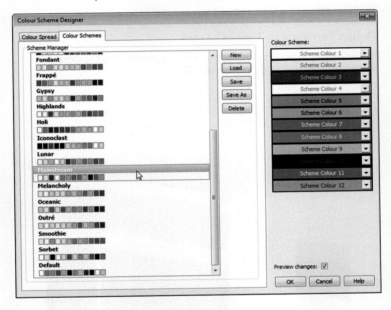 **Colour Scheme Designer** on the default context toolbar.

2 From the dialog's **Colour Schemes** tab, double click a colour scheme from the list (or select and click **Load**), then click **OK**.

🔖 For more information on **Colour Schemes,** please see the *Using colour schemes* topic in the help, or why not try the *WebPlus Colour Schemes* tutorial!

Colour Schemes

WebPlus offers an impressive selection of pre-designed **Colour Schemes**, which you can apply to your own site or use to update a **Design Template** or **Theme Layout**.

The following pages provide previews of the pre-designed **Colour Schemes** provided with **WebPlus X5**.

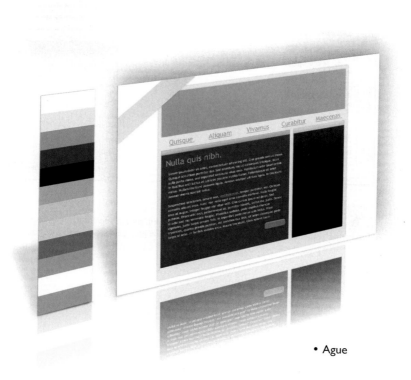

• Ague

• Comic

• Coral

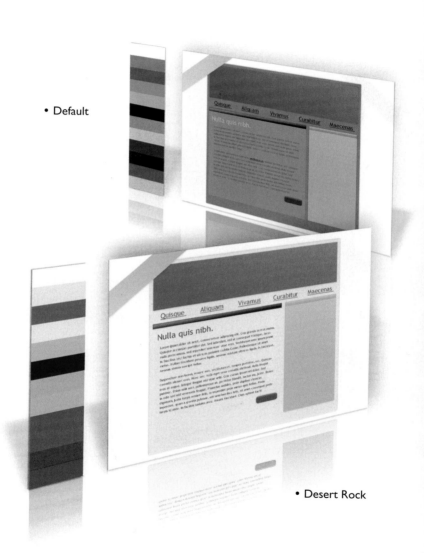

• Default

• Desert Rock

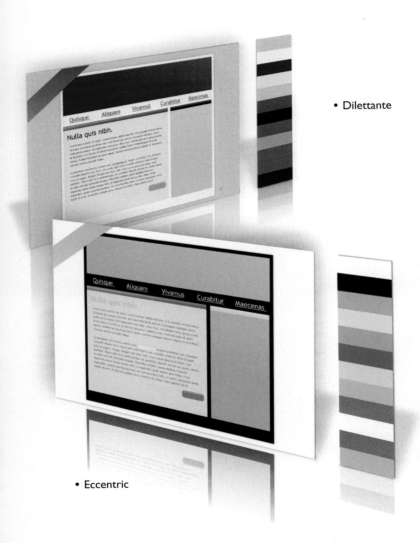

• Dilettante

• Eccentric

• Fawn

• Fondant

• Frappé

• Gypsy

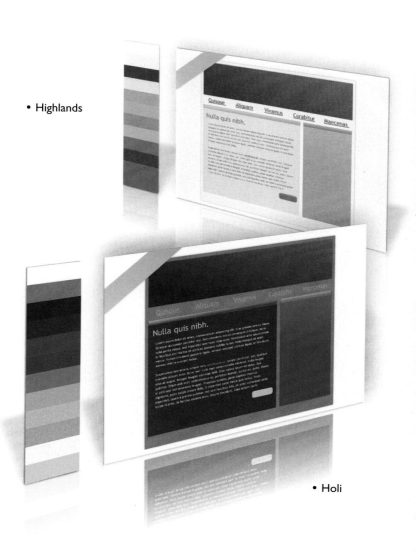

• Highlands

• Holi

• Iconoclast

• Lunar

• Mainstream

• Melancholy

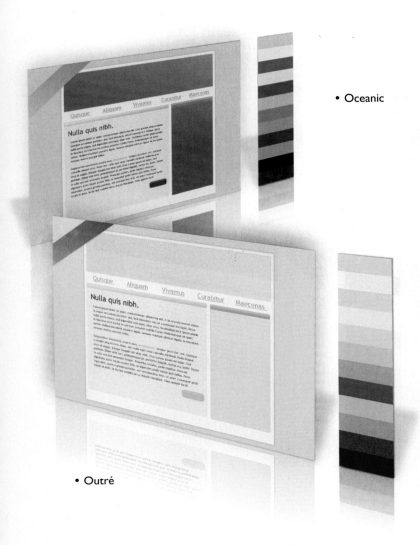

• Oceanic

• Outré

• Smoothie

• Sorbet

4 WebPlus Gallery

WebPlus Gallery

The WebPlus **Gallery** can be found on the right-hand side of the workspace, and provides a selection of designed elements that can be used in your own sites.

The following categories of elements are available from the WebPlus **Gallery**:

- Badges & Stickers
- E-Commerce Buttons
- Flags
- Flash Banners
- Icon Sets
- Icons
- Logos
- Notes
- Picture Frames
- Quick Symbols
- Quotes
- Ribbons
- Smilies

The following pages provide previews of the new **Gallery** content provided with WebPlus **X5**.

Pre-designed elements which have been schemed will update inside the gallery when you change your colour scheme!

Badges

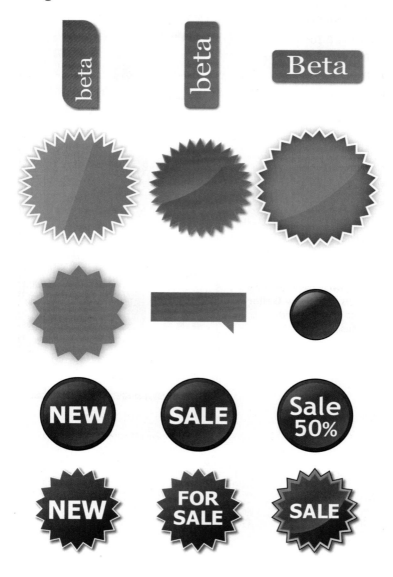

Stickers

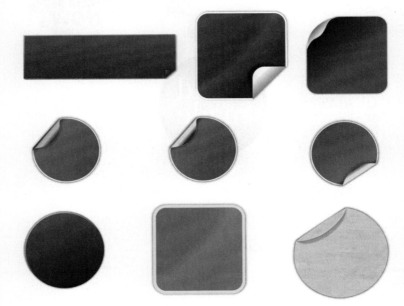

Add To Cart

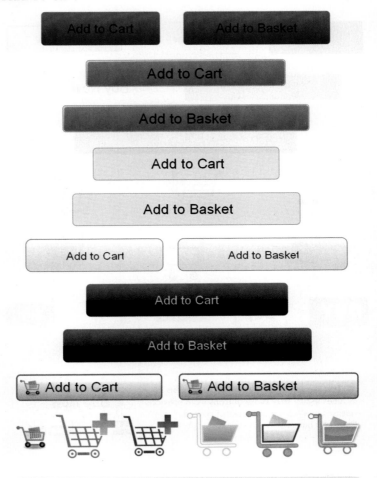

This section of the WebPlus Gallery also includes legacy **Add To Cart** buttons from previous releases of WebPlus and a set of related **PayPal**® buttons.

Buy Now

This section of the WebPlus Gallery also includes legacy **Buy Now** buttons from previous releases of WebPlus and a set of related **PayPal**® buttons.

Donate

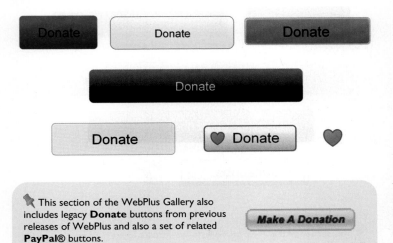

This section of the WebPlus Gallery also includes legacy **Donate** buttons from previous releases of WebPlus and also a set of related **PayPal**® buttons.

Search

This section of the WebPlus Gallery also includes legacy **Search** buttons from previous releases of WebPlus.

Subscribe

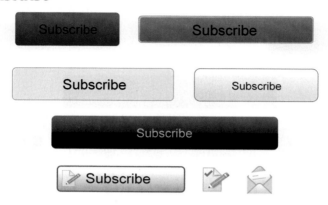

This section of the WebPlus Gallery also includes legacy **Subscribe** buttons from previous releases of WebPlus and a set of related **PayPal®** buttons.

Unsubscribe

View Cart

🔖 This section of the WebPlus Gallery also includes legacy **View Cart** buttons from previous releases of WebPlus and a set of related **PayPal**® buttons.

Begin Checkout

Bright

Button

Dark Grey

Light Grey

Schemed

Standard

💡 The print icons in the icons sets supplied in the WebPlus Gallery have print actions already applied to them!

For more information on actions please see the Help topic *Applying Actions*.

Business

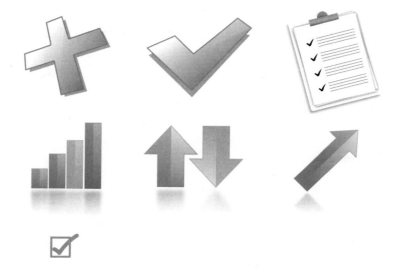

Contact

Hospitality

Business

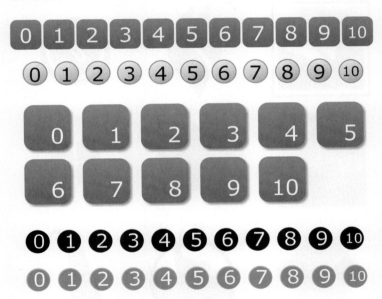

Ratings

Logos

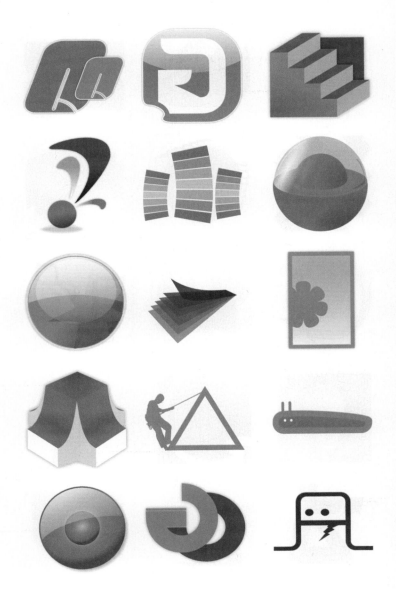

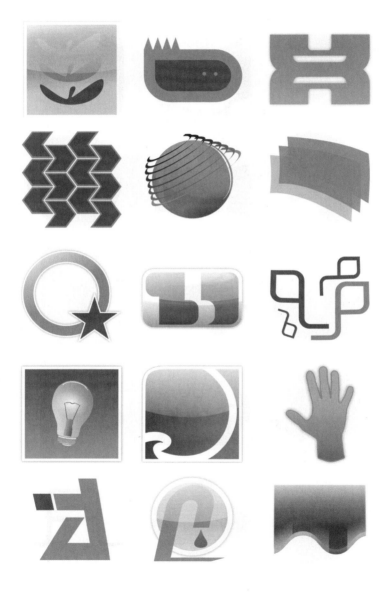

As mentioned in the introduction to this chapter, some of the objects included in the **WebPlus Gallery** are schemed. This means that if you change your site colour scheme then the colours of schemed items will also update.

All of the **Logos** included in the **WebPlus Gallery** are schemed, so they will all update to any colour scheme you choose, they will even show a preview of the new scheme in the **Gallery** tab!

Notes Extras

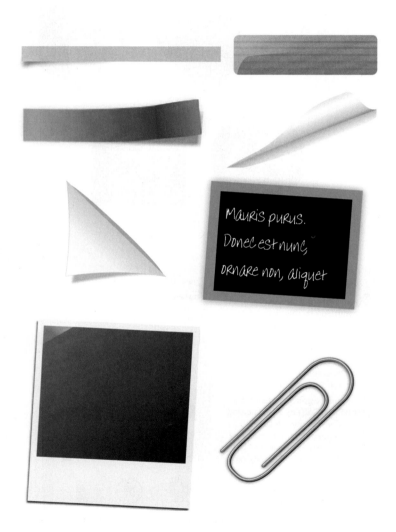

Notes Panels

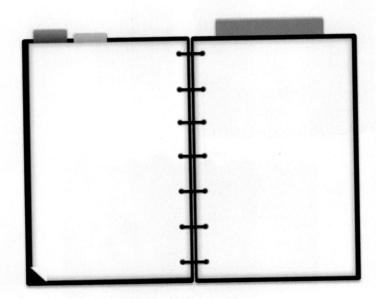

Notes

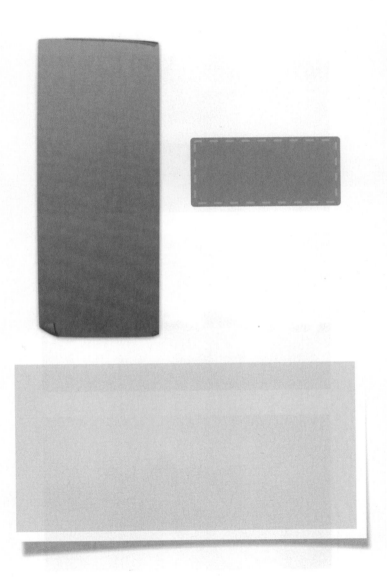

Essentials

Quotes

6 6 9 9

" "

6 6

Vestibu lum
semper enim
non eros. Sed
vitae arcu.
Aliquam

9 9

Vivamus justo

Nulla quis nibh. Proin ac pede vel
ligula facilisis gravida. Phasellus
purus Etiam sapien. Duis diam
urna, iaculis ut, vehicula ac varius
sit amet, mi. Donec id nisl. Aliquam
erat volutpat

Vestibulum semper enim non eros. Sed vitae arcu.
Aliquam erat volutpat. Praesent odio nisl. suscipit at.

Morbi pellentesque mauris interdum porta t incidunt
neque orci molestie mauris vitae iaculis dolor felis at nunc.

In eget sapien vitae massa rhoncus lacinia. Nullam at leo
nec metus aliquam semper. Phasellus tincidunt, ante nec

Morbi pellentesque mauris interdum porta ti ncidunt
neque orci molestie mauris vitae iaculis dolor felis at nunc.

Nulla vestibulum
eleifend nulla.

In hac habitasse platea
dictumst. Mauris rutrum

In eget sapien vitae
massa rhoncus

Nulla vestibulum
eleifend nulla.

In hac habitasse platea
dictumst. Mauris rutrum

In eget sapien vitae
massa rhoncus

In hac habitasse platea

Vestibulum semper eros.

"Vestibulum velit orci, bibendum eget, molestie eu, sagittis non, leo. Nullam sed enim. Duis ac lorem. Lorem ipsum dolor sit amet, consectetuer adipiscing elit. Suspendisse potenti. Sed tincidunt varius arcu."

Nulla vestibulum eleifend nulla. Suspendisse potenti. Aliquam turpis nisi venenatis non accumsan nec imperdiet laoreet lacus. In purus est mattis eget imperdiet nec.

Maecenas condimentum

Aliquam dapibus ipsum vitae sem. Ut eget mauris ac nunc luctus ornare. Phasellus enim augue, rutrum tempus, blandit in,

03

Morbi Pellentesque Mauris

Pellentesque

Maecenas condimentum
Vestibulum vel tellus. Sed vulputate. Morbi massa nunc convallis a commodo gravida tincidunt sed turpis.
Maecenas lorem
Aenean euismod iaculis dui. Cum sociis natoque penatibus et magnis dis parturient montes, nascetur ridiculus mus.
Nulla quam
Aenean fermentum, turpis sed volutpat dignissim, diam risus facilisis nibh, sit amet iaculis est turpis non tellus.

Ribbons

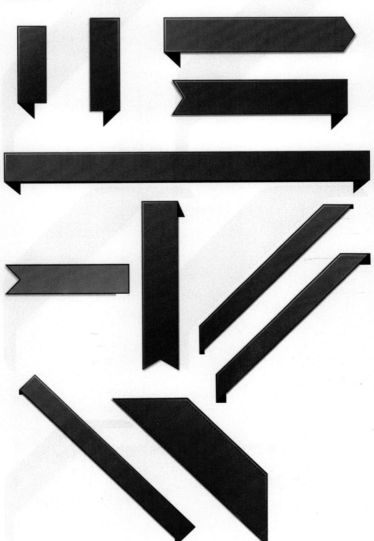

Why not add text to your ribbons?

Made in WebPlus

5 Theme Layouts

Theme Layouts

WebPlus provides a selection of **Theme Layout** templates that you can use as starting points for your own sites.

Available from the Startup Wizard, the **Theme Layouts** offer a range of layout styles. Each layout comes complete with picture and text placeholders, and offers a choice of purpose-built site pages.

To open a Theme Layout:

1   In the **Startup Wizard**, click **Create > Use Design Template**.

2   In the **Create New Site From Template** dialog:

- Browse the **Theme Layouts** category and select the layout you want to use.

- Choose a colour scheme from the drop-down list.

  You can choose from three schemes specially designed to complement the theme layout, or you can apply any of the other colour schemes included with WebPlus.

- In the **Pages** pane, using the check boxes, choose the site pages to include in the layout.

- Click **Open**.

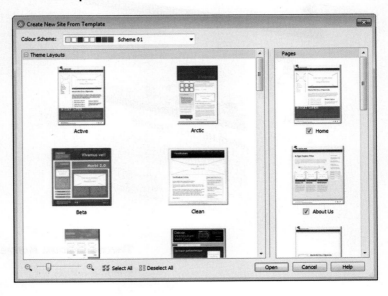

The following pages provide previews of the **Theme Layout** templates provided with **WebPlus X5**.

Theme Layout: Active

- Home
- About us
- Products
- Gallery
- Contact Us

- Article 01
- Article 02
- Links
- Terms & Conditions

Theme Layout: Arctic

- Home
- About us
- Products
- Gallery
- Contact Us

- Article 01
- Article 02
- Links
- Terms & Conditions

Theme Layout: Beta

- Home
- About us
- Products
- Gallery
- Contact Us

- Article 01
- Article 02
- Links
- Terms & Conditions

Theme Layout: Clean

- Home
- About us
- Products
- Gallery
- Contact Us

- Article 01
- Article 02
- Links
- Terms & Conditions

Theme Layout: Clouds

- Home
- About us
- Products
- Gallery
- Contact Us

- Article 01
- Article 02
- Links
- Terms & Conditions
- Search Results

Theme Layout: Décor

- Home
- About us
- Products
- Gallery
- Contact Us

- Article 01
- Article 02
- Links
- Terms & Conditions

Theme Layout: Doodle

- Home
- About us
- Products
- Gallery
- Contact Us

- Article 01
- Article 02
- Links
- Terms & Conditions

Theme Layout: Eco

- Home
- About us
- Products
- Gallery
- Contact Us

- Article 01
- Article 02
- Links
- Terms & Conditions

Theme Layout: Editorial

- Home
- About us
- Products
- Gallery
- Contact Us

- Article 01
- Article 02
- Links
- Terms & Conditions

Theme Layout: Ledger

- Home
- About us
- Products
- Gallery
- Contact

- Article 01
- Article 02
- Links
- Terms & Conditions

Theme Layout: Mode

- Home
- About us
- Products
- Gallery
- Contact Us

- Article 01
- Article 02
- Links
- Terms & Conditions

Theme Layout: Natural

- Home
- About us
- Products
- Gallery
- Contact Us

- Article 01
- Article 02
- Links
- Terms & Conditions

Theme Layout: Nature

- Home
- About us
- Products
- Gallery
- Contact

- Search Results
- Article 01
- Article 02
- Links
- Terms & Conditions

Theme Layout: Pop

- Home
- About us
- Products
- Gallery
- Contact Us

- Article 01
- Article 02
- Links
- Terms & Conditions

Theme Layout: Shabby

- Home
- About us
- Products
- Gallery
- Contact Us

- Article 01
- Article 02
- Links
- Terms & Conditions

Theme Layout: Solid

- Home
- About us
- Products
- Gallery
- Contact Us

- Article 01
- Article 02
- Links
- Terms & Conditions

Theme Layout: Spiro

- Home
- About us
- Products
- Gallery
- Contact Us

- Article 01
- Article 02
- Links
- Terms & Conditions

Theme Layout: Tabs

- Home
- About us
- Products
- Gallery
- Contact Us

- Article 01
- Article 02
- Links
- Terms & Conditions

Theme Layout: Tickle

- Home
- About us
- Products
- Gallery
- Contact Us

- Article 01
- Article 02
- Links
- Terms & Conditions

Theme Layout: Vintage

- Home
- About us
- Products
- Gallery
- Contact

- Article 01
- Article 02
- Links
- Terms & Conditions

6 Pro Templates

Pro Templates

WebPlus provides a selection of **Pro Templates** that you can use as starting points for your own sites.

Available from the Startup Wizard, the **Pro Templates** are categorized templates containing royalty-free pictures which can be adopted to fast-track you to your completed site. You just need to personalize placeholder text, then publish!

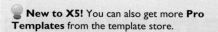 **New to X5!** You can also get more **Pro Templates** from the template store.

Visit: **http://go.serif.com/Templates/WPX5**

To open a Pro Template:

1 In the **Startup Wizard**, click **Create > Use Design Template**.

2 In the **Create New Site From Template** dialog:

- Browse the **WebPlus X5 Pro Templates** category and select the template you want to use.

- Choose a colour scheme from the drop-down list.

  You can choose from three schemes specially designed to complement the template, or you can apply any of the other colour schemes included with WebPlus.

- In the **Pages** pane, using the check boxes, choose the site pages to include in the layout.

- Click **Open**.

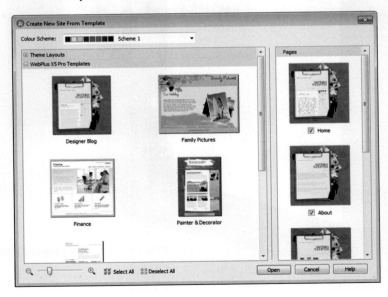

The following pages provide previews of the **Pro Templates** provided with **WebPlus X5**.

Pro Template: Designer Blog

- Home
- About
- Portfolio
- Contact
- Terms of use

Pro Template: Family Pictures

- Holiday
- The Kids
- About Us
- Contact

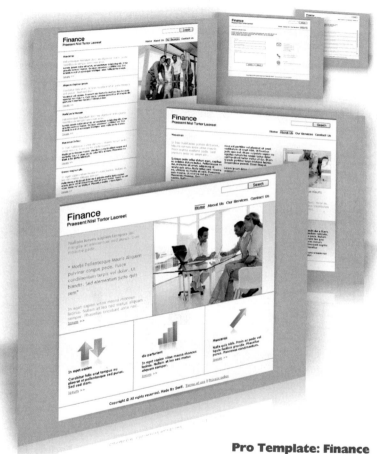

Pro Template: Finance

- Home
- About
- Our Services
- Contact Us
- Search Results

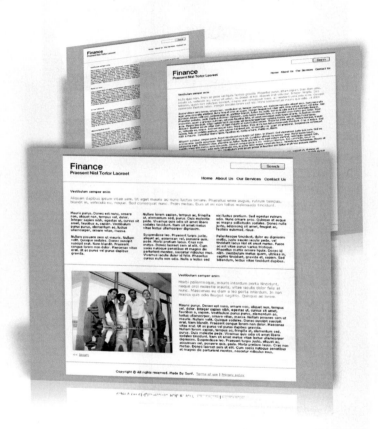

- News Story
- Terms of use
- Privacy Policy

Pro Template: Painter & Decorator

- Home
- About
- Services
- Contact

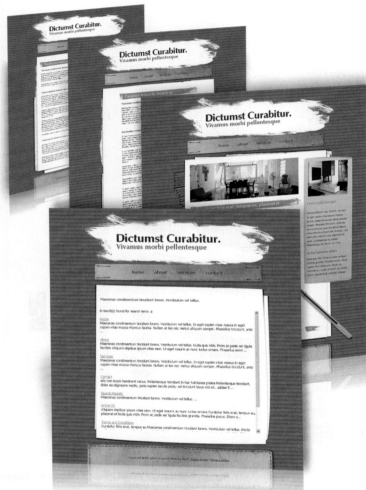

- Search Results
- Article 01
- Terms and Conditions
- Privacy Policy

Theme Layout: Real Estate - Business

- Home
- About
- Properties
- Contact
- Search Results